A FALLEN STAR

The Murder of Ebenezer Parker and Execution of Joseph Drew

A True Story

By
Lori-Suzanne Dell

Writers Dream Publications.
Brunswick, Maine. 2023.

Copyright Page

Published by
Writer's Dream Publications.
22 Baribeau Drive, #116.
Brunswick, ME. 04011.

Manufactured in the United States of America.

Library of Congress Control Number: 2021915631
Names: Dell, Lori-Suzanne, 1964-Author.
Title: A Fallen Star. The Murder of Ebenezer Parker and Execution of Joseph Drew / by Lori-Suzanne Dell.
Description: Brunswick, Maine, Writers Dream Publishing, 2023.
Identifiers: LCCN 2021915631|
ISBN (Hardcover) 9798481750675
ISBN (Paperback) 9781077956605|
ASIN: (Kindle) |
ISBN-

Dedication

In so much as our American Democracy is defined by its laws, which guard our rights, privileges, and responsibilities, our law enforcement officers are the domestic protectors and enforcers of those laws. Thereby, they are our nation's domestic guardians of democracy.

I dedicate this manuscript to all of the Fallen Stars, our law enforcement officers, who gave and continue to give their lives to protect the United States of America. And, I offer my heartfelt appreciation to each man and woman, past and present, who stands this watch.

The cemeteries of today are well-worn with the footprints of those who have searched for the people who came before us. Someday, the cemeteries of eras yet to come shall be well worn with the footfalls of those who shall come, searching for us all.

– Lori-Suzanne Dell

Table of Contents

Mission Of The Historian's Inquiry.
Introduction By Sheriff Kevin Joyce.
Foreword By Historian Ron Romano.
Author's Note.
Chapter One: A Young America In Chaos.
Chapter Two: Levi Quinby.
Chapter Three: Ebenezer Parker.
Chapter Four: Joseph Drew.
Chapter Five: With Malice, Aforethought.
Chapter Six: Cold Nights, Painful Days.
Chapter Seven: Just The Beginning.
Chapter Eight: The Trial Of Joseph Drew.
Chapter Nine: The Trial of Levi Quinby And
                         The Sentencing of Joseph Drew.
Chapter Ten: 25 Men And Many Prayers.
Chapter Eleven: The Execution Of Joseph Drew.
Chapter Twelve: The Aftermath.
Chapter Thirteen: The Parkers Of Cape Elizabeth
                         and The Widow Mary Parker.
Chapter Fifteen: A Historian's Inquiry Begins.
Chapter Sixteen: The Smoking Gun.
Chapter Seventeen: Another Process Of Elimination.
Chapter Eighteen: Probing The Long Parker Lot.
Epilogue
Acknowledgments
Bibliography/Sources Used.
Photo/Image Credits
About the Author

A FALLEN STAR

The Murder of Ebenezer Parker
And Execution of Joseph Drew

This is a true story

The Mission of the Historian's Inquiry

Historian's Inquiry
To locate the grave of Cumberland County

Ebenezer Parker

On April 25th of 2002, Maine Department of Public Safety
Deputy Commissioner John Rogers wrote a memorandum to then
Cumberland County Sheriff Mark Dion requesting that his
department locate the graves of any of the department's fallen
officers for recognition in the Maine Law Enforcement Memorial
annual remembrance, as required by Maine law. This seemingly
simple request unwittingly sparked a nearly two-decades-long search
for the final resting place of Maine's first fallen law enforcement
officer killed in the line of duty, Cumberland County Deputy Sheriff
Ebenezer Parker.

Since then, the search for the grave of Deputy Parker has
engrossed two separate Sheriff's Office Administrations, and the
assistance of other law enforcement officials, historians,
genealogists, librarians, historical societies, town and city clerks, and
many interested citizens, who have all scoured the archives, libraries,

cemeteries, vital records, and numerous area histories, to solve a mystery which harkens back more than two-hundred and fifteen years, to the days – some dozen years – before Maine became a state in 1820.

The story of this Fallen Star is a true tale. Through the historian's inquiry that was formed, I have endeavored to locate as many primary source materials, such as maps, birth records, death certificates, burial listings, and marriage records, as could be located, as well as church records and other vital statistics. And, I have compiled numerous secondary sources, such as newspaper articles, obituaries, diary entries, letters, and references to the people, places, and events herein recorded. I have also compiled several stated facts and related information from many book publications and websites, to fill in the blanks and sculpt as true and full a picture of the story as could be told. In the end, it came to me to compile the information, sort through the details, determine fact from confusion, and develop the theories that allowed us to refocus the research and uncover the details which have – until now – been hidden or lost for over two-hundred years. This endeavor has produced as true and as complete a story as can be told, as best as we know it.

The line of duty death and murder of Deputy Ebenezer Parker, the trial and execution of his killer, and the mystery of Parker's final resting place is still relevant today. This story sheds light upon the history of the early days of a young United States of America in the years before Maine had become a state when it was still the Massachusetts District of Maine. And, it tells of a bygone era when law enforcement in America was still developing and the criminal justice system was ever transforming from the old British System of Law first enacted and transformed into the American system of justice that we have today.

This is the story of a man who lived in that bygone era, his witnessing of history, his duty to his state, his community, and his family, and the details of his death and the trial and execution of his killer. And, this book is a story of the present-day historian's inquiry to solve one of the oldest and most beguiling of unsolved mysteries in the history of the United States, New England, and the State of Maine.

Introduction

By Cumberland County Sheriff Kevin Joyce.
Photo: Courtesy of the Cumberland County Sheriff's Office.

Today, when a law enforcement officer, a firefighter, a member of Emergency Medical Services, or a member of the military is killed in the line of duty, their personal sacrifice is honored by giving the deceased a "hero's funeral" and burial service. Oftentimes, when a first responder is killed in the line of duty, the deceased is escorted everywhere his/her body goes and is never left alone, even at the funeral home, until the officer's burial. This is known as "standing watch." The individual receives the highest honors for their ultimate sacrifice.

A line-of-duty death funeral is usually attended by fellow first responders and/or active and retired military personnel, some of who travel great distances to honor the deceased. In addition to a traditional funeral program, there are usually bagpipers present to play ritual funeral songs such as *Amazing Grace* and *Coming Home.* There is a 21-gun salute, in some cases a rider-less horse, in other cases the casket is carried on a wagon, fire truck, or other public safety vehicles to honor the individual's sacrifice.

Typically in modern times, the funeral procession is escorted by police officers on motorcycles, in police cruisers, and with other public safety vehicles in the procession, such as ambulances and fire apparatus. The aforementioned are usually lined up in the procession following or escorting the hearse. At some point, a funeral procession will likely go under the extended ladders of two fire department ladder trucks, displaying an American flag, then along the route, and over any roadway overpasses. Citizens and first responders usually line up to pay tribute to the deceased. Sometimes, when appropriate, there is a fly-over of aircraft to acknowledge the service of the deceased. Finally, upon the burial of the deceased, the agency that lost the individual who was killed in the line of duty pays particular attention to honoring the hero's service and sacrifice each year, either during Law Enforcement Memorial Week, on Memorial Day, or National Firefighter Memorial week.

In the early 2000s, the Cumberland County Sheriff's Office, in Portland Maine, received two grave markers and two small State of Maine flags from the Maine Chiefs of Police Association, which were sent in order to be placed on the graves of the two Cumberland

County Sheriff's Office deputies that had been killed in the line of duty.

I had been employed by the Cumberland County Sheriff's Office for nearly 20 years when we received these two grave markers. Until then, I had not heard about the two Cumberland County Deputy Sheriffs that had given the ultimate sacrifice, their lives. The names of the two Cumberland County Deputy Sheriffs killed in the line of duty are listed on the National Law Enforcement Memorial Wall in Washington, D.C., and on the Maine Law Enforcement Memorial Wall, in Augusta. Yet, as an agency, we never took the time to recognize their sacrifice.

At that time, I took on the mission to locate the final resting place or burial ground of these two deputies and to place the grave markers and flags on their respective graves. It turned out to be quite a challenge.

A quick Google search of the internet provided me with information on the death of Deputy E. Dean Pray of Windham, who was killed in the Town of Windham, Maine on August 20, 1940. Deputy Pray was a part-time deputy who also owned and operated a motor vehicle repair facility near the intersection of Routes 302 and 115, in an area otherwise known by Windham locals as Boody's Corner. Deputy Pray was approached by two individuals who were later identified as members of the Jehovah's Witness Church. After a brief altercation, Deputy Pray was shot to death.

Through some research, and having the luxury of knowing some of the descendants of Deputy Pray, I was able to locate Deputy

Pray's final resting place, inside the Manchester Cemetery, on Route 302 in Windham, just feet from where Deputy Pray was viciously killed.

In the early 2000s, the Cumberland County Sheriff's Office held a ceremony as we placed the grave marker near Deputy Pray's gravestone, for the very first time. We were fortunate enough to have members of the Pray family present as we honored Deputy Pray's sacrifice once again. Since then, the Cumberland County Sheriff's Office places the grave marker and a Cumberland County Sheriff's Office flag on Deputy Pray's grave every May, in honor of Law Enforcement month.

The second deputy, who was the first deputy killed in the line of duty at the Cumberland County Sheriff's Office, and the first deputy killed in the line of duty in what was then known as the State of Massachusetts (now the State of Maine), was killed in 1808. This search proved to be a much more difficult task.

Known as the ultimate Cumberland County Sheriff's Office "Cold Case," I and others at the Cumberland County Sheriff's Office have been working on locating the final resting place of Deputy Ebenezer Parker for over a decade. In all of my research, I located very little information on Deputy Parker. In fact, I found more information on Deputy Ebenezer Parker's killer, since he was one of several capital punishment cases resulting in the suspect being hanged to death in the early 1800s, in Maine.

Our research was comprised of several personal visits to various libraries, conversations with members of the numerous historical societies in Cumberland County, walks through some of Cumberland County's older cemeteries, and visits to the Latter-Day Saints Genealogy Center in Salt Lake City, Utah. We also perused various antique books about Cumberland County and Portland, written in the 1800s and 1900s.

Fortunately, on May 10, 2019, I received an email from Lori-Suzanne Dell, a historian, and author from Brunswick, Maine who was interested in our search for Deputy Ebenezer Parker's grave and she offered to help us with our research. Her offer to conduct some research, along with her expertise as a historian, was welcomed.

Ms. Dell has worked diligently and tirelessly on finding the final resting place of Deputy Ebenezer Parker. She has also requested the assistance of other historians including Ron Romano, an author, and historian of cemeteries, most notably the historic Eastern Cemetery in Portland, Maine. And, she invited the assistance of James Rowe, at the time the President of the Cape Elizabeth Historical Preservation Society, among others.

Like any "Cold Case", any time that you can acquire additional resources and expertise to solve the case, it is a wise decision. Through Ms. Dell's extraordinary efforts, we were able to locate and begin a dialogue with some extended members of Deputy Parker's family in the Midwest who were unaware of the sacrifice that their early family ancestors had made in 1808.

There is no evidence of a typical line-of-duty death funeral, like the ones held today. There is not even an indication of a headstone to celebrate Deputy Parker's existence, never mind his

14.

service and sacrifice. There is no written documentation that Deputy Parker's funeral service was anything like the line of duty death honors we provide today.

As you will see, Ms. Dell was able to locate numerous pieces of a puzzle - a puzzle that had many missing pieces. However, now with her work, and this book, even though we may not definitively know where Deputy Ebenezer Parker's body was laid to rest, we can shed light on Deputy Parker's sacrifice and keep his memory alive for centuries to come.

Kevin Joyce

Sheriff, Cumberland County, Maine.

April 10, 2023.

Foreword

By Maine Historian Ron Romano
Photo: Courtesy of Ron Romano.

Maine has thousands of historic burial places, from backyard plots of colonial settlers to multi-acre spaces developed by local communities. Some are true "graveyards" (or "churchyards"), patches of ground adjacent to a church and reserved for the devoted. Others consist of public land set aside for the townspeople to bury their own, usually called "burying grounds." Today, we tend to use the word "cemetery" to describe them all.

Every cemetery holds secrets. Records of burials may have been lost over time, erroneously recorded, illegible, or never even written down in the first place. Families that marked their graves with a stone may have assumed that the stone itself would suffice, perhaps unaware that over time natural deterioration, neglect, vandalism, and other factors would take a toll and all but erase the record created at the time the stone was placed. The result? Thousands upon thousands of graves are now "lost," with no burial records or gravestones known to confirm them.

Those of us who consider ourselves historians—and indeed fortunate enough when others see us the same way—are by nature investigators. We cast a wide net, gather facts and uncover secrets, sort them, arrange them, and then carefully put them together in such a way as to create the "Aha!" moment we crave so much. The discovery of something "new" is well worth the effort; a dead end or brick wall can be frustrating, confounding, and disappointing.

Lori Dell contacted me as she was beginning her journey for this book about the 1808 murder of Deputy Ebenezer Parker and the execution of his killer Joseph Drew. She'd seen my brief accounting of the event in my book about Portland's historic Eastern Cemetery, where Drew was featured as one of five men who were hanged for murder and presumed to be buried there. Her question was simple enough: *"Do you know where Ebenezer Parker is buried?"*

Thus began my role in Lori's journey to discover the final resting place of Deputy Parker. We shared theories and discussed possibilities. I may not have met a historian more determined. Lori sees each dead end as a challenge to find another path and each brick wall as an opportunity to break her way through it. Sometimes her dogged determination pays off.

17.

As you'll read, Deputy Parker was an unsung hero. It was his killer who grabbed the headlines and his execution launched *his* name into infamy. Rev. Samuel Deane wrote just two words in his diary on May 26, 1808: "Drew tried." But it's the parenthetical remark by William Willis, the publisher of the Journal in 1849, that speaks volumes. It reads "Joseph Drew, for killing a man at Saccarappa..." A man! With no mention of Parker's name or position, it was again Drew being remembered 40 years after their deaths. So, it is with thanks to Lori that Parker finally receives the spotlight he deserves.

No gravestones have yet been found for either. Rest in peace, Joseph Drew. And rest in peace, Deputy Ebenezer Parker.

Ron Romano

Author's Note

What you are about to read is the entire story, a true story, as best I can determine it. The story is the culmination of over four full years of historical research that has included information from the California Coast to the Mid-Atlantic States and from the southern Gulf Coast to the Canadian border. Thousands of files, from newspapers, maps, documents, vital records, genealogies, histories, and many more books and records, have been scoured and sifted-through to uncover every nugget and morsel of information that could be found. In the end, each piece of information, each date, each name, all combined like pieces of a jig-saw puzzle to weave a storied picture that uncovers a view into a mystery that has remained hidden for more than two-centuries. And, it all began with one simple question, "Where is the final resting place of Cumberland County Sheriff's Deputy Ebenezer Parker?"

Lori-Suzanne Dell
April 2023.

19.

Chapter One

The EMBARGO.

A Young America In Chaos

On April 18th of 1806, the Congress of the United States of America passed an Embargo Act to forbid foreign trade between all European nations and the United States. Great Britain and France had been deeply embroiled in a great Napoleonic War for the past three years, which saw many American merchant ships caught-up in the melee. In an effort to stop goods and supplies from reaching their enemy, both European Nations would regularly stop all American merchant ships bound for enemy ports, seize the cargo as war contraband, and then arrest certain American sailors of dubious citizenship and impress them into the military service of that seizing nation. Despite America's declared neutrality in the European chaos, and over the full-throated objections of President Thomas Jefferson, the seizures and impressments of American citizens continued unabated. Jefferson desperately wanted to avoid any conflict which could force America into choosing a side in the European nightmare, and that could force the United States to declare war. The Embargo Act was set into law to disrupt these international high-seas events by stopping all out-bound shipping from the United States. The effect of this embargo was then re-enforced by the Embargo Act of 1807. Unfortunately, the combined financial effects of the embargo devastated the trade-dependent economy of a still-young America.

The Nation of the United States was just seventeen states young by 1806, and the country stretched mostly along the eastern coastline from the Carolinas to the northern Massachusetts District of Maine, and from the Atlantic Ocean westward to Ohio, Tennessee, and Kentucky. Jefferson's purchase of the Louisiana Territory in 1803 had greatly expanded, nearly doubling, the size of the United States. However, these new and raw frontiers were still being explored and mapped by 1806 and the embargo only slowed the eventual rush for westward expansion. The embargo affected every state and territory of the United States, either directly or indirectly. Yet, no area was more greatly affected than the eastern seaboard with its many seaports, shipping hubs, wharves, communities, cities, and harbors.

Most Americans engaged in some common trade or profession as a prime means for making a financial living. Many men worked as carpenters or shipwrights, sailmakers, distillers, shoemakers, weavers, loggers, blacksmiths, sawyers, or as fishermen, seamen, livestock drovers, merchants, dock hands, or general laborers. The more educated were employed as printers or lithographers, bankers, doctors, ministers, lawyers, teachers, or politicians. Most, regardless of wealth or the lack thereof, engaged in some extent of farming, either for commercial means or private use. Many had some interest in shipping, either as merchants or investors, or as shipbuilders, sailors, or suppliers. In all, nearly every manufactory or agricultural enterprise relied on income from international trade, which could only be made possible through shipping. As long as ships were moving goods and supplies the economy of America and the financial fortunes of Americans were also moving and successful prosperity was growing. The Embargo Acts of 1806 and 1807 brought all of that success to an abrupt end.

In Maine, harbors, ports, and wharves were suddenly overflowing with ships normally at sea transporting cargo from America to foreign ports of call. Every slip and mooring point was full and the harbor had little room for another ship to squeeze in. Augusta, Portland, and Bath had the most prominent shipping ports in Maine at the time, and Portland was the sixth-largest shipbuilding center in the United States. Despite the importance of these three harbor cities, all three came to a standstill and their harbors became full parking lots for static ships with nowhere to go. The docks of the harbors in the District of Maine all became stacking places for cargo, waiting to be loaded into the holds of brigs, schooners, and sloops. In the northeast, lumber, rope, sail, textiles, agricultural foods, iron, munitions, and other goods and supplies, made up the bulk of New England's trade exports. Meanwhile, in the middle and southern states, corn, wheat, tobacco, salt, sugar, molasses, cotton, rice, indigo, grain meals and flour, and other staples, became their prime export. Now, with the Embargo of 1806 in place, these would-be exports clogged the wharves, rotted on the docks, and decayed in the cargo holds of docked ships that were prohibited from leaving port for foreign trade destinations.

Worse yet, towns and cities all across the young United States came to an immediate standstill as men who would have otherwise been busy harvesting crops, producing goods, logging timbers, transporting or loading ships, or working in mills or textile manufactories, suddenly had no jobs, nothing to do, and no income to support themselves or their families as The United States of America fell into a deep and immediate economic depression. Foreign trade exports in America had topped $108 million before the Embargo took effect. Within one year, American Foreign Trade had lost 75% of its value, slipping to just $22 million. Unemployment was rampant and thoroughly widespread. Unpaid debts, both personal and professional had skyrocketed and had no boundaries. From the wealthiest of individuals to the most financially stable businesses, to the most prominent citizens, and down to the most ordinary man, the rising debt had overtaken nearly every family, in every community, and in every state and territory.

Those who held debts did all they could to collect from those who owed the debts. Many sought to sell off anything they had to raise funds enough to pay off what they owed. Yet, there was little money had by anyone to buy anything and much of what was sold off was let go for just a mere fraction of its actual value. This left the debtor with little of any value and still facing the immediate demands for a settlement of debts. And, the person holding the note of debt was now left with little alternative for recouping his monies.

The American System of Law in 1806 was still a system much like the English System of Law that had ruled the former British Colonies before the American Revolution. Although the system of law was being altered by the American Congress and new laws were being written and introduced, it was a long process to replace the former English System of Law with a new codified System of American Laws. In most cases, the court system itself was still being set into place and jurisdictions were still being created. When a holder of unsatisfied arrears wanted the law to step in and collect the unpaid debt they would first seek an attorney, much like we still do today. The attorney would then create a written notice to the debtor demanding the debt be immediately settled within a specified period of time. When the debt still went unsatisfied the lawyer would seek an order from the Court of Common Pleas to justify that the debt was indeed owed and allow the debtor one more chance to pay up. Should the debtor still be unwilling or unable to pay what he owed the lawyer could seek the order of the court to be enforced. At this point, the County Sheriff would be handed a writ for the demand of payment. A deputy would then take the writ to the debtor, demand payment, and either be paid in full, which would bring the entire matter to a swift end, or the deputy would be forced to arrest the debtor and haul him off to jail. The arrested debtor would often be carted away in chains and shackles, much to his humiliation, in full view of the public. He would then be placed in debtors jail where the debtor would remain until the satisfaction of his debt was made, either by payment or by the sale of his possessions which would be seized by the deputy and auctioned off. The proceeds of the auction would then go towards payment of the debt, legal fees, and the cost of the deputy's service.

By 1807, the international situation between France, Great Britain, and the United States, had gotten dramatically worse. Desperate shipping merchants and seamen all along the eastern seaboard were openly defying the Embargo Act and risking long and perilous voyages across the Atlantic to trade with either France or Great Britain. Either of these war-weary countries were happy to receive fresh goods and supplies by any means they could and welcomed the American merchant ships. The other country was not so happy to see their enemy resupplied with goods or materials that would be used against the other. Thus, further enforcement to stop trade with the enemy was stepped up by both Napoleon I and King George III.

For Mainers, defying the Embargo Act seemed to be a responsibility some felt was their duty as Americans to perform. Quietly and secretly loading their ships in the dead of night and then slipping quietly out of the harbor under the cloak of darkness saw several ships disappear from the Harbor Master's count at sunrise. Most saw sailing to France or England far too risky, even for duty-bound citizens. Yet, a quick trip to the open borders of Canada, Labrador, or even as far as the Bahamas, Portugal, or other more southern ports of call meant money could be made. Yet, these Maine ships who defied the Act and sailed with full loads risked a great deal. Even though many remained close to the American shore, and far from the French or British coasts, they still risked capture and impressments. Even American Naval vessels were not immune from these seafaring attacks.

By June, the American Warship USS Chesapeake was sailing along the United States coast just off the shores of Norfolk, Virginia, when she came under attack by the British Warship HMS Leopard. The Chesapeake was caught completely unaware and was overwhelmed by the might of the superior British Warship, and the Leopard's crew forcibly boarded the Chesapeake. Four American sailors were taken prisoner, tried as deserters of the British Navy and one was hung for his alleged crime. The Leopard then released the Chesapeake and returned to Great Britain with three new "impressed" crew members. Americans seethed with anger at the news of the naval outrage off the coast of Virginia and calls for war with Great Britain grew louder with each passing day. This was exactly what President Thomas Jefferson, by forging the Embargo Acts, had desperately tried to avoid.

Thomas Jefferson and Congress both struggled to quell the inflamed international incident through intense diplomatic efforts, yet Great Britain had little sympathy for America's objections, and the British claim to a right of impressments only continued unimpeded. Jefferson had little choice: He either had to go to war with Great Britain or turn up the legislative heat. But, America was in no position to wage a war, across the Atlantic Ocean, in Europe. There was no standing army in the United States, only groups of state-controlled militia, and the nation only had a small and little-prepared navy. Jefferson's only reasonable alternative was legislative.

President Jefferson's Embargo Act of 1807 was passed in congress by November and it reinforced the Act of 1806, further calling for a more enforced prohibition of international shipping and trade and restating America's neutrality in the European conflict. The American economy had already reduced most proud Americans to a population of shamed paupers, and the reinforcement of the Embargo only worsened the nation's financial matters. Sawmills, gristmills, and blacksmith shops were closing all across the nation. Textile manufactories were shuttered and distilleries were abandoned. Ships clogged seaports even more so than before and were left unmanned at moorings in harbors, and tied to wharves and docks, all along the eastern seaboard. Loggers closed their camps and sent their lumberjacks home. Shipyards once bustling with the sights and sounds of hundreds of men building new ships to meet a huge shipping demand now sat idle, silent, and still. And, the cargo that had waited for loading on the docks and wharves of America's seaports, or in the holds of ships, now prohibited from leaving the harbor, continued to rot in the spring rains, bleach out in the hot summer sun, and completely decay and foul the air with a peculiar miasma. Men without jobs and little else to do wandered the streets aimlessly, stood around talking to other static-bodies, or imbibed in an alcoholic-induced passing of time, each man worrying for his family, concerned with a coming winter, and were left wondering when all the bitter misery would finally come to an end.

Court cases involving debt in America had dramatically increased in late 1807. And, lawyers' writs, foreclosures, public sale auctions - held by County Sheriff – and dispossessions, had also increased markedly. While the rest of America was out of work, the need for more Sheriff's deputies had increased, as did their reputation for being the harbingers of bad news, enforcers of dispossession, and punishers of the poor. American frustration with the economic disaster that had befallen them had grown from worrisome to weary, and from annoying to angering. The economic crisis was now a financial crisis of chaos and the patience of these early Americans had been nearly exhausted. Vocal outrage turned to vocal defiance, then to physical opposition. Soon, men were publicly warning debt holders and their collectors, including law enforcement, from taking action. In Augusta, where the lumber trade was decimated by the financial effects of the embargo, Sheriff's Deputies were busier than ever before enforcing the collection of debts and many of the residents had had enough. A group of angry locals took a page from history and mirrored the Boston Tea Party by dressing as Indians. Wherever Sheriff's deputies arrived to enforce the collection of debts this band of would-be natives also showed up. The would-be tribe confronted the law agents and prevented the collections from taking place. Threats of force and other violence ensued and soon the militia was called upon to assist the deputies in enforcing the law. Similar acts of civil disobedience and disruption occurred in other areas and counties of the District of Maine, as well as in Massachusetts and the United States. In fact, the problem had become so prevalent in Maine and Massachusetts that Massachusetts Governor James Sullivan issued orders of compliance, which were printed in newspapers throughout the Commonwealth, warning citizens not to interfere with the lawful duties of law enforcement.

Meanwhile, public outcry for relief had outgrown the ability of communities to cope with the financial crisis. Poor farms, the predecessor to today's homeless shelters, were over-full and turning people away. Churches in towns and cities, especially in New England, were setting up the nation's first soup kitchens, and overall need had quickly outstripped overall supply. And, the demand for settlement of debts had not diminished as more and more families were seeing their homes and farms, and all of their possessions auctioned off. Many families were cast out of their homes, off of their lands, and were being made dependent on what little community assistance or family help was available. Winter was fast approaching and, for many who had no family to help, the survival of their wives and children left many a husband and father in frantic straits and desperate for any means of immediate satisfaction.

As December of 1807 approached, time – it had seemed – had run out, and there was no promise of relief being offered by the government, local community heads, or church leaders. The war in Europe, between France and Great Britain, still showed no signs of ending anytime soon. And, worst of all, the brutal reckoning of a cruel and frigid New England winter had begun, as the frost had descended, and snow had already fallen. Everyone, especially in the greater area of Falmouth – in present-day Portland - were praying for their own Gideon, someone to deliver them from all the misery and heartache they were enduring. People were praying for a hero, someone to strike back, someone to help to bring all of their sufferings to an end.

Chapter Two

Levi Quinby

By late 1807, many of the inhabitants of Cumberland County, in the northern Massachusetts District of Maine, were out of work or barely employed and were all in some amount of debt. One of these men to find himself in the desperate straits of indebtedness was Levi Quinby of Saccarappa (Westbrook). And, Levi was not the only one of the vast Quinby clan to fall on hard financial times.

This branch of the Quinby family came to Saccarappa in about 1770, when Benjamin Quinby, a clothier from Somersworth New Hampshire, relocated to Cumberland County, Maine, to be closer to his twin brother Joseph. By then, Benjamin's son Nathan was about fourteen years old and was busy learning the clothier trade from his father who had opened a shop on Maine Street in Saccarappa Village. The family was said to have lived on the northerly side of Maine Street, in the "Holy Ground" district. By

1778, Nathan had married Azuba "Rosina" Partridge and the couple had six children, three sons, and three daughters. Nathan and Rosina's son Levi was born in Saccarappa (Westbrook) in about 1780.

By 1803, Benjamin sold to his son Moses a fourth ownership in a gristmill, located on the falls at Presumpscot in Saccarappa. Three years later, in 1806, Moses then purchased a dye house, a fulling mill, and other accessories, also on the falls. The Quinby clan had become a large and prominent family that branched out through the areas of Saccarappa, Stroudwater, Falmouth Neck, and as far north as Brunswick.

Captain John Quinby, Benjamin's brother, had settled in Stroudwater, an area between Saccarappa and Portland, where he had built a shipyard on the Fore River, and he had become wealthy, not only from shipbuilding but, from the actual shipping industry as well. His two sons, Moses and Levi (often confused with their Saccarappa cousins), were both young men building names for themselves. Moses entered the profession of law, while his younger brother Levi became a merchant with a shop located on the wharf at Portland.

Three of Captain John Quinby's nephews, Frederick, Thomas, and Henry, had relocated to Brunswick while still children, after the death of their father Joseph. Their mother had re-married, this time to Amos Lunt of Brunswick, and the boys were then raised in the northern portion of Cumberland County. By 1803, Henry Quinby was appointed as the Postmaster of Brunswick, a position which only seems to have lasted a year. By 1804, both Henry and Frederick were listed as "Traders," and had relocated soon after to Falmouth (Portland).

Nathan's branch of the Saccarappa Quinby's had become well invested in water rights on the Presumpscot River, and all had family interests in the Quinby mills, all located at the falls, as well as the clothier shop on Main Street. It seems, when reading the history of this Quinby clan, that a picture of a heavily financially-invested and industrious family is presented. And, it seems that Nathan's young son Levi, along with his cousins Frederick and Henry, were engaged together in at least a few business interests. Among some of these interests was a sawmill in Brunswick, various land deals in Cumberland County, and interest in a small Saccarappa blacksmith's shop located just across the road from the family mills at the Falls.

By 1806, as the Embargo was beginning, the Quinby clan fell into immediate trouble. The war in Europe, between France and England, had already had a damaging impact on Captain John Quinby's shipping interests. Less than a decade earlier, on July 7th of 1797, Quinby's ship the "Eunice" – named for his daughter – was seized by a French Privateer ship, L'Intrepide. The Eunice had just unloaded in Liverpool, England, and then reloaded with British merchandise bound for the more posh shops of New York and Philadelphia. When Eunice was seized her Master, Captain Thomas Seal – John Quinby's nephew – was taken prisoner and later released and returned home. But, the Eunice, and her cargo, was kept by the French government as a prize of war. Fortunately, lists tell of nearly twenty ships built by the Quinby and Lewis yard at Stroudwater, and at least six were still being profitably operated by Quinby and Lewis employed Captains as cargo vessels engaging in international trade.

Sadly, Captain John Quinby had contracted consumption, as early as 1804, and by September 27th of 1806, Captain John Quinby had died at Stroudwater. Although his business partner, Archeleus Lewis, would continue for some time, Quinby's death placed his great shipping business at risk. While their father's wealth was divided equally among all three of his children, the business debts of their father, which were considerable, were divided among the two sons, Moses and Levi. And, soon after Quinby's death, the Embargo Act of 1806 took effect on the Maine economy. The death of John Quinby, followed by the Embargo, was a two-punch combination that served a gut-punch to the Quinbys of Stroudwater. Men had to be laid off from the shipyard and orders from suppliers had to be cut. Financial times, even for the solvent Stroudwater clan of the Quinby's would require serious belt-tightening to get through.

Captain John Quinby's nephews, Frederick and Henry, had found themselves in a great deal of financial hot water. The decline of profits from the interests in the family sawmill at Brunswick, as well as any interests they had in the Saccarappa Blacksmith's shop, and lost proceeds from their many speculative land deals, soured their hopes for turning smaller investments into greater profitable ventures. The lands they had purchased, with hopes to quickly resell, had required these two brothers to borrow large sums of money. And, with mills falling idle and silent everywhere, their revenue stream had also fallen silent and idle. Quickly, lenders grew impatient, and merchant creditors everywhere began calling in their debts. It seems that Henry and Frederick had engaged many friends and relatives in their investment schemes and many of the schemes had begun to fail even before the embargo had taken place. As early as 1803 Frederick Quinby and Daniel Conant were co-defendants in a suit in the Cumberland County Court of Common Pleas, the equivalent of today's small claims court. Henry and Frederick Quinby are noted in many dozens of such cases in the Court Record from 1803 through 1808, and many of the cases involved other co-defendants. Eventually, by about 1805, the brothers lost their mill and lands in Brunswick when the Sheriff of Cumberland County took the properties on the execution of a court order to settle debts they owed. Also, in 1805, shortly before the death of their uncle John Quinby, the brothers had sold properties they held in Portland to raise sums of cash. Once their possessions in Brunswick were taken, the brothers moved back to Westbrook and the warm embrace of the Quinby family.

Henry and Frederick's cousin, Levi Quinby of Saccarappa, was also a Quinby in debt by 1806. Any paying interests he had in the family businesses on the Presumpscot River appear to have dried up. With a stagnating economy, the clothier shop isn't believed to have earned much, if anything. And, any family wealth that had years before been received from the inheritance of the late Captain Jesse Partridge, may also have been gone. Levi had by now gone to work as a laborer, in his Uncle Moses' mills on the Presumpscot, and at the blacksmith shop, just across the road on Main Street, which was owned by Frederick Quinby's friend and co-defendant Daniel Conant. Levi was no longer a man of position in Saccarappa, but a mere laborer in the family businesses. And, he had gotten into debt with a local merchant and trader named Josiah Gould. Gould appears to have been a man to who many, many, people were indebted. As the Embargo ravaged the economy from 1806 to 1808, Josiah Gould also appears in the records of the Cumberland County Court of Common Pleas in many dozens of cases, most often as the plaintiff seeking to recover a debt. By late 1807, Josiah Gould held a note of debt for Levi Quinby and Levi was, as it appears, doing everything he could to avoid Josiah Gould.

Chapter Three

Ebenezer Parker

By 1807, the local economy in the District of Maine had only grown worse and the town of Cape Elizabeth was hit hard. Located just across the harbor from Falmouth Neck, Cape Elizabeth had been a great community of seafarers, chandlers, merchants, ship builders, carpenters, fishermen, farmers, and much more. The area was originally settled around 1630, despite early raids by Native Americans, harsh and challenging weather, and many, many hard economic times. Before 1776, Cape Elizabeth was officially chartered in 1765 as part of a young Cumberland County, which was itself a part of the Massachusetts Bay Colony, all under the control of the nation and government of Great Britain. And, Maine itself was just a province of the northern area of the Massachusetts Bay Colony. Fishing and shipbuilding were prominent industries for the area, which was steadily growing with new inhabitants, most of whom came from the Massachusetts areas of Cape Cod, Truro, and

New Gloucester, as well as many other New England, seafaring, communities.

In 1734, brothers Joseph and Elisha Parker came to Cape Elizabeth from Truro, Massachusetts, to settle and build the first meeting house building of the Congregational Church on what would become known as Meeting House Hill. Joseph and Elisha bought lands on and surrounding the Meeting House, and they began a business on the edge of the harbor where they engaged in the operation of a ferry, and owned a small shipyard. There, at Cape Elizabeth, their families grew. By 1756, Joseph's son Nathaniel, a housewright like his father, married Hannah Roberts, also of Cape Elizabeth, and their family began. In 1758, their first child – a son - John Parker was born, followed by their second son Ebenezer in 1760. Then, three daughters; Rebecca (1761), Hannah (1763), and Sarah (1765), were all born at Cape Elizabeth. Nathaniel and Hannah's family were well underway and more were yet to come.

Before 1771, Joseph Parker had acquired one-hundred acres of land in the town of Gorham, just a few miles to the west of the Cape Elizabeth border. In his sixty-fifth year, he sold the land, known as lot #30, to his son Nathaniel and his wife Hanna. The couple then quickly moved their young brood to Gorham, built a home, began a farm, and started a new life at Gorham. However, within just a few years these plans of a simple farming life at Gorham were thrown into chaos. Difficult relations with the colonial rule of Great Britain were giving colonial subjects serious fits. Heavy taxation on goods, little to no say in their governmental rule, and annoyance with the hard-fisted rule of King George III and England's Parliament began a furor that swept through the colonies. Soon, prominent men from every portion of British-controlled North America were meeting to officially object to the treatment of the colonies and to try to find some good ground for compromise. Instead, these well-meaning men found themselves tangled with an obstinate monarch and a less-than-sympathetic Parliament. Words meant to reconcile and calm only separated and infuriated a distant government. The attempt to quell a growing conflagration only burned slowly out of control. Soon, peace failed as threats ensued. Loyalty to the King turned to disgust for the Crown. It wasn't long before words waned and bullets were fired. When word came to Cape Elizabeth, and Gorham, of the melee at Lexington and Concord, in Massachusetts, it was clear to everyone that an American Revolution had begun. Suddenly men were needed to form militias, in all areas of the British Colonies, to defend their homeland from their own ruling government and their own ruling King. By the fall of 1775, young brothers John and Ebenezer Parker were both seventeen and fifteen, respectively, and both were eager to defend their homes and take part in a great adventure for independence.

On October 18th of 1775, a British contingent of warships returned to Falmouth, what is today Portland Harbor, to exact a measure of revenge for a previous incident. That spring, local militia under the leadership of Brunswick Tavern-Keeper and Militia Commander Samuel Thompson, had arrested His Majesty's

Lieutenant Henry Mowatt, a commander of a British ship of war, the HMS Canceaux. Mowatt was sent to enforce trade between British merchant suppliers and locals, but a colonial boycott had been employed and Thompson intended to enforce the act of defiance. While Mowatt was onshore arranging church services for his crew Thompson's Militia arrested Mowatt. The second in command of the Canceaux threatened to fire his cannons on the town if the ship's commander was not immediately released. But, Thompson refused to acquiesce to the threat. Local authorities met to discuss the matter and it was soon decided that Mowatt should be immediately released. Thompson was ordered to release Mowatt and eventually did so, but Mowatt was livid and swore he would have his revenge.

John Parker and his younger brother Ebenezer had signed on as volunteers with a local Gorham militia unit to serve at the Seacoast Defense located at Cape Elizabeth's Fort Hancock, (what is today Fort Preble, in South Portland).

PARKER, EBENEZER. Private, Capt. David Strout's co.; enlisted July 17, 1775; discharged Dec. 31, 1775; service, 5 mos. 27 days; company stationed on seacoast at Cape Elizabeth and Scarborough; also, 1st Sergeant, Capt. Briant Morton's co.; entered service Jan. 27, 1776; service to Sept. 1, 1776; company stationed on seacoast at Cape Elizabeth and Scarborough; also, Capt. Morton's co., Col. Mitchel's regt.; service from Sept. 1, 1776, to date of discharge, Nov. 25, 1776, 2 mos. 25 days; company stationed on seacoast at Cape Elizabeth and Scarborough; also, Capt. Reuben Butterfield's co.; engaged Dec. 16, 1776; discharged March 16, 1777; service, 90 days; 15 days (300 miles) travel home also allowed; also, Capt. John Wentworth's co. of matrosses, Col. Peter Noyes's regt.; company mustered by Col. Noyes May 20, 1777, and stationed at Fort Hancock, Cape Elizabeth.

From the United States Rosters of Revolutionary War Soldiers, 1775-1783.

The defending contingent was on hand to guard against any attempt by the British to land soldiers on the Cape Elizabeth shore. Also, the Seacoast Defenders were there to guard a kept herd of cattle that grazed nearby. Locals were sure the fresh-meat-starved British sailors would surely try to confiscate the livestock to replenish their own food stores on board the Canceaux. The Parker brothers, and the Seacoast Defenders, were on high alert as they saw Mowatt's small fleet sail into the Harbor on the morning of October 18th. Mowatt had returned and this time he wanted revenge.

Mowatt's vessels took position along the shoreline of the harbor with their guns facing Falmouth Neck (Portland). Mowatt's Flagship HMS Canceaux carried sixteen cannons and took up a center point in the line. Canceaux was flanked by the HMS Cat and her twenty cannon, the HMS Halifax and her twelve cannon, the HMS Spitfire and her eight cannon, and all the ships were resupplied as necessary by the accompanying HMS Symmetry. Mowatt disembarked the Canceaux with a marine guard and they began plying broadside posters in the city. Then, Mowatt met with city officials and gave them the bad news. He warned the local officials that the citizens of Falmouth had just two hours to flee the city. Officials pleaded with Mowatt for his mercy, but to no avail. Mowatt told these prominent men of Falmouth, these former loyal subjects of the Crown, that their punishment was about to be delivered by order of their King. Mowatt warned that time was wasting; in just under two hours he would order his ships to open fire and a detachment of his men would torch the town. Mowatt then returned with his men to the HMS Canceaux.

Word spread quickly through Falmouth Neck, as residents scurried to take up their belongings, gather their loved ones, and warn their neighbors. Approximately ten-thousand citizens, some revolutionary colonials and some Loyalists to the Crown, with their arms and wagons filled with everything they could gather, then ran for their lives. When the two hours were over Mowatt's warships opened fire.

The bombing of Falmouth Neck illuminated the nighttime sky, and from Cape Elizabeth, may have appeared similar to this lithograph. Image courtesy of the Maine Historical Society.

For the next six hours, a total of fifty-six cannons fired continuously, over and over, into the city. Shell and shot sailed overhead and whistled through the sky, exploding into homes, businesses, warehouses, open ground, trees, and anything that stood in the way. The sounds of explosions and the crackling of shot, as they tore through wooden structures, pierced the air. Smoke filled the sky and blotted-out the sun as the smell of burning homes and livelihoods wafted across Falmouth Neck. Where shot failed to set fire to buildings Mowatt's men succeeded as they walked the town with their burning torches. On the outer periphery of the peninsula, in the area of what we today know as Deering Park, many of the Falmouth neck inhabitants stood helplessly. Surrounded by their belongings, their family, friends, and impotent city leaders, these thousands watched the flames devour everything they knew as home as their ears filled with the sounds of each shell as it was fired, sailed through the air, and crashed into its target, their faces aglow with the reflection of the red radiance of flames that illuminated the smoky scene. Across the harbor, in Cape Elizabeth, all the Parker brothers could do was remain with their militia unit and watch the total destruction unfold.

By six that evening, Mowatt finally felt vindicated. His revenge was complete. When he finally ordered his ships to cease fire there were few targets left to fire at. The entire peninsula that was Falmouth was completely engulfed in flames. Mowatt's torch-crew climbed back aboard their ship and the British sailors stood and watched as their work consumed everything in sight. Then, Mowatt gave the order and the small British fleet lifted anchor, and sailed out of the harbor and into Casco Bay while the entire City of Falmouth Neck burned behind them. John and Ebenezer watched as the warships once again passed by Fort Hancock. Doubtless, many fired shots from their muskets in hopes of finding a target to harass. But, the ships were too far away and the range of their rifles was not nearly enough to cause any harm. The lateness of day saw a sky, that had earlier been darkened by torrents of black smoke, now darkened by the coming of night. Yet, the sky was now filled with the glow of illumination from the burning fires of homes, businesses, and the personal possessions of every inhabitant of Falmouth Neck. It is believed that the militia men then boarded the Parker family ferry and crossed the harbor to help fight the fires.

By July 4th of 1776, the Declaration of Independence had been signed and word spread that the nation of the United States of America had been born and officially separated from the tyrannical rule of Great Britain. John and Ebenezer, as well as their father

Nathaniel, had all signed on to fight for the independence of America. Nathaniel had signed up with the Continental Army and remained for three years of service. John had signed on with McLellan's Company in Gorham and remained in service until about 1779.

Meanwhile, young Ebenezer remained with the Seacoast Defenses at Fort Hancock, in Cape Elizabeth, and was likely charged to remain behind to care for his mother and seven sisters who remained inland, on the farm at Gorham. During his service, while Ebenezer remained behind to guard Cape Elizabeth and care for the family, John had taken part in numerous battles including the Penobscot Expedition,

44.

and Bagaduce Expedition, which sought to re-take control of much of the down east coast of Maine from the British. And, both John and his father Nathaniel had ended up in winter camp at Valley Forge, in Pennsylvania.

When the war ended on September 3rd of 1783, John and Nathaniel had both returned home safe and sound. Ebenezer was released from the Seacoast Defenses at Cape Elizabeth and mustered out of service with the rank of Sergeant. Nathaniel was likely happy to be home with his wife and daughters and to get back to work on the farm. John returned to his farm in Durham, where his wife Elizabeth Warren Parker, and their children welcomed him home with open arms. It is believed that Ebenezer also returned to the farm in Gorham to work alongside his father to bring the family farm back up to snuff. Yet, for both John and Ebenezer, it seems they still hungered for the adventurous life they had been living for the past eight years. Now, remaining at home, on their farms, seemed to hold little interest for either brother.

The post-war economy had taken off and soared after the peace was announced in 1783. In fact, the needs of Great Britain, which caused them to colonize the New World in the first place, continued unabated. The great natural resources of the American continent still held great and vast interest for England. Lumber, iron, agricultural produce, tobacco, and the many other staples available from the new United States of America now became a new economy for the young country and Great Britain now became America's biggest customer, as did France and the rest of Europe, the West

Indies, and the rest of the civilized world. American ships formerly required for war were now repurposed for trade and orders for new ships to be built had skyrocketed and caused a great surge in new shipbuilding businesses to spring up in coastal communities all along the eastern seaboard of the United States. Cape Elizabeth, Falmouth Neck, and Stroudwater, all became local hotbeds of shipbuilding, and each of those ships built, once ready for sea, required crewmen to sign-on and sail the seas, transporting cargo to waiting customers who had formerly been enemies or allies of the new and emerging United States. Great adventures and lucrative pay awaited men who signed on to man these ships and take to the high seas, and both John and Ebenezer likely saw an opportunity to better provide for their families, and their own futures, all while living new and great adventures. John and Ebenezer wasted no time in signing up and going to sea, to serve and work together again.

By 1787, John and Ebenezer were not far off the coast of England, sailing and working together. It is not known on what ship they served, or who they sailed under. However, it is possible they served on a ship owned by the Parker family, and maybe Captained by their father's cousin, Ebenezer Parker. Captain Ebenezer Parker is believed to have been the son of Elisha Parker, one of the two Parker brothers who came to Cape Elizabeth from Truro Massachusetts. Not much is known about this side of the family who were born and raised at Cape Elizabeth before the town became organized in 1765. Yet, the evidence at hand surely indicates that these Parkers were a tough lot, a family who – much like the Quinbys - stuck together.

And, there is a likelihood that Captain Ebenezer was commanding a ship built by the Parkers at Cape Elizabeth. Regardless of the details, tradition reports John Parker was lost at sea just off the coast of England in 1787. He was just twenty-nine years old. Certain documents submitted by John's widow, Elizabeth Warren Parker, confirm this loss at sea.

By 1789, just two years after John's death at sea, his father Nathaniel was visiting his late son's farm in Durham. He was presumably there to look after his daughter-in-law, his grandchildren, and their family farm. Nathaniel appears to have been splitting his time between the family farms in Gorham and Durham, and it was taking a toll on the man who was not yet fifty-four years of age. Suddenly, Nathaniel died at his son's farm in Durham and the Parker family now had no adult male present to lead the large and extended family. With Nathaniel and John both gone, the twenty-seven-year-old Ebenezer Parker was now the man of the family. But, it is believed that Ebenezer was still at sea working to make money to send home. His responsibilities now included two farms, his mother, his seven sisters, his sister-in-law Elizabeth and her widowed mother, as well as Elizabeth and John's five children. All in all, there were at least fifteen people, mostly women and young children, who now needed a provider and a protector. And, trouble was brewing in Gorham. It was time for Ebenezer to come home.

By 1790, records indicate that Elizabeth Warren Parker and her five children, plus her widowed mother, had left the farm in Durham. Without the help of Nathaniel life on the Durham farm was too difficult to manage. Elizabeth and her children left Durham and moved to Gorham to stay on the Parker farm with Hannah and her daughters. But, the extended Parker family of "widows and orphans," were not faring well without a responsible adult male to assume legal responsibility, and to provide for the needs of this large clan at Gorham. It appears that some sort of assistance was required by the town to help these women make ends meet. On May 13th of 1790, the Gorham Town Selectmen (Stephen Longfellow, Samuel Elder, and James Phinney) issued an order directing the local Constable to warn and remove Elizabeth Warren, her mother, and her children, off of the Parker farm and out of the Town of Gorham.

> Cumberland ss. To the Constable of the Town of Gorham
> L. S. in s^d County, Greeting.
>
> You are in the name of the Commonwealth of Massachusetts directed to Warn, And give notice unto Kezia Whitney—Elizabeth Parker, the Wife of John Parker Deceas^d and her Family—together with her Mother, the Widow Warren,—John Poland & Family,—William Holmes—Joseph Wakefield & Family—Joseph Young Junr—Charles Caveno & Family—Gideon Snow—Joshua Swett—Turff Thomas—Mary Goodwin—Reuben Libby—& James Brackett, Who have lately come into this Town, for the purpose of abiding therein, not having obtained the Town's Consent therefor. That they depart the limits thereof with their Children & others under their Care, (if such they have) within fifteen Days.——And of this Precept with your doings thereon you are to make return into the office of the Clerk of the Town, within Twenty Days next coming, that such further proceedings may be had in the premises as the Law directs,——Given under our hands & seals at Gorham aforesaid this Thirteenth Day of May, A. D. 1791.
>
> STEPHEN LONGFELLOW)   Selectmen
> SAMUEL ELDER   }   of
> JAMES PHINNEY   )   Gorham.

A Transcription of the Gorham Order of Dismissal as it appears in the *History of Gorham*, by William McLellan.

The order gave these Parkers fifteen days to leave town. The Parker family was in trouble yet it appears that Ebenezer had arrived home just in time, had ended his days at sea, and set his attention to quelling the family troubles. He assumed responsibility for the family, took control of the farms, and ended the unsympathetic order of the Town of Gorham.

Elizabeth Warren Parker's eldest son Nathaniel was now old enough to assume legal responsibility for his family and he was capable of taking over the duties of the family farm. But, Ebenezer still had a responsibility to his brother's family. As the family patriarch, Ebenezer still had to permit the marriage of his niece Elizabeth. While Ebenezer was attending to his family, and the extended Parker family, he was also engaging in the business of a "trader" and he was making several land purchases and sales, as well as working the Gorham farm. By 1804, Ebenezer's sisters were all married and living with their husbands, and his widowed mother Hannah Roberts Parker was also marrying a Cape Elizabeth businessman named Benjamin Fickett. When Hannah left the Gorham farm to live with her husband at Cape Elizabeth nearly all of the Parker clan were now gone from the Gorham Farm. One Parker sister however remained on the Parker farm. Ebenezer's sister Mary, known as Polly, and her husband William Riggs, took over the family farm at Gorham and remained there, and raised a family of their own. The farm remained in the Riggs family for many years to come.

By as late as 1804, Ebenezer Parker had moved back to Cape Elizabeth and he began seeing a woman named Mary Larrabee, of Scarborough Maine. Her brother Thomas had married Ebenezer's sister Anna and they had purchased a farm just a few doors down the road from Elizabeth Warren Parker and the Durham farm. And, with Ebenezer's help, Mary's nephew, William Larrabee, married Elizabeth Warren Parker's daughter, Elizabeth Parker. Ebenezer was also able to make a deal for a farm that was located right in between the Parker and Larrabee farms in Durham, just for William and Elizabeth. But, Ebenezer had to finance the deal and carry the note for the young couple. Now, with all of his responsibilities to the large Parker family concluded, Ebenezer had just one thing left to do before he proposed to Mary Larrabee.

Ebenezer had success as a trader, but the times were getting tough and the profits of these ventures had seriously diminished. Local newspapers were filled with pages of articles and commentary on the European War, and reports of the actions that both Congress and President Thomas Jefferson were taking in Washington. Ebenezer, like many at the time, no doubt saw that more harsh times were coming. If his life had taught him anything, he must have known he had to be prepared for anything. By 1805, Ebenezer Parker took on a job that, despite the rough economic times which undoubtedly lay ahead, could well provide for him and his planned family at Cape Elizabeth. This employment was not dependent on a profitable trade, nor was it reliant on a good economy. No matter how bad the economy might get he could be assured of a weekly salary and financial security for his family. Ebenezer Parker accepted a position as a Deputy with the Cumberland County Sheriff's Office.

On April 17th of 1805, Ebenezer Parker and Mary Larrabee were married by the Reverend William Gregg at the Congregational Church, which Ebenezer's Grandfather Joseph Parker and Great Uncle Elisha Parker had built – some seventy years before – on Meeting House Hill in Cape Elizabeth.

By the early winter of 1806, just nine months after their wedding ceremony, Mary Larrabee Parker gave birth to her first son Nathaniel Charles Parker at Cape Elizabeth. It appears that Ebenezer and Mary, and now with their first son in tow, were probably living in the home of Captain Ebenezer Parker and his wife Esther Higgins Parker. And, it appears that Esther was not in good health and that Mary may have been caring for the nearly seventy-year-old Esther. Captain Ebenezer appears to have been retired from the sea since about 1793 when his father Elisha had died. Elisha's brother Joseph had died in 1774, and with both brothers gone many of their children appear to have left Cape Elizabeth. At least two of Captain Ebenezer's brothers had left Cape Elizabeth and moved eastward to Penobscot County to engage in shipbuilding near Steuben, Maine.

Form R-2 (For old records only)

COPY OF AN OLD RECORD OF A MARRIAGE

Groom ___Ebenezer Parker___
Bride ___Mary Larabee___
Residence of Groom ___Cape Elizabeth Me.___
" Bride ___Cape Elizabeth Me.___
Age of Groom ___
" Bride ___
Color of Groom ___W___
" Bride ___B___
Occupation of Groom ___
" Bride ___
Birthplace of Groom ___
" Bride ___
No. of Marriage of Groom ___
" Bride ___
Groom Widowed or Divorced ___
Bride " " " ___
Intention Filed ___Nov. 3, 1804___
By whom Married ___William Gregg___
Residence ___Cape Elizabeth Me.___
Official Station* ___Clergyman___
Date of Marriage ___Apr. 17- 1805___
Place ___Cape Elizabeth Me.___
*Clergyman, Justice of the Peace, etc.
(Record continued over)

51.

Once again, it seems the welfare of the Parker family was again in the sole hands of the younger Ebenezer Parker, who himself was now approaching his mid-forties. With a wife and a son, and now two elderly Parkers to care for, Ebenezer's work as a Cumberland County Deputy Sheriff may have been supplementing the Parker family at Cape Elizabeth.

By December of 1807, the second Act to strengthen the Embargo of 1806 took hold. The economy had only gotten worse since the first enactment of the embargo, just a year before. Debts had grown greatly in America, and in the District of Maine, and the effort by lenders and debt holders to recoup their losses had redoubled. The claims brought forth in the Cumberland County Court of Common Pleas had become massive and the execution of warrants, seizures, and debt collections was overwhelming the efforts of sheriff's deputies in counties throughout Maine and the United States. And, the Cumberland County Sheriff's Office, appears to have had about thirty deputies working at the time in communities throughout the huge County.

Come Christmas Day in 1807, Esther Parker's health had taken a downward turn. Two days later, on December 27th of 1807, Esther Parker died in Cape Elizabeth. She was sixty-nine years old. The Congregational Church was operating without a regular minister, one hired to specifically handle the matters of the church, since Reverend William Gregg had left the Pastorate in 1806. Now, Reverend Caleb Bradley, himself the Pastor of the Stroudwater Parish, was giving double duty by covering the Cape Elizabeth congregation, until a new minister was hired for the church at Cape Elizabeth. Bradley was undoubtedly called upon for Esther's funeral, and in most cases, funerals at the time were held within two days of the person's death.

On December 29th, Esther's funeral was held, most probably in the mid to latter part of the day, to allow people time to travel and pay their respects before the internment services. Yet, despite the family's sadness Deputy Parker still had a duty to perform, and he traveled to Saccarappa early that morning. He was holding an issued warrant for the arrest of Levi Quinby for an outstanding debt called-in by Josiah Gould. Parker had located Quinby, arrested him in Saccarappa, and then remanded Quinby into the authority of Richard King, a man

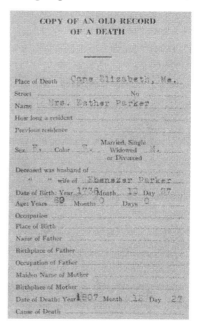

who may have been a deputy, a jailer, or constable, with some authority to detain a prisoner. Parker then made his way back to Cape Elizabeth for the funeral services of Esther Parker. Presumably, Parker intended to return after the services and gather up his prisoner and take him to the Cumberland County Jail, on Congress Street, at Falmouth Neck. But, when Parker returned to gather-up his prisoner he learned that "Old Dick" King had allowed Quinby to go free, with a promise to immediately settle his debts or to surrender himself upon request if he should fail to settle the legal matter. For the next two weeks, Deputy Parker went about both his family and his professional business and gave little concern to Levi Quinby. Two weeks seemed an adequate amount of time for Quinby to settle his legal woes and his financial arrears to Gould.

On Monday January 11th of 1808, Deputy Ebenezer Parker awoke to a dark and frosty morning. There were morning chores to be done. Firewood needed to be brought in to see Mary through the day. The cow needed milking, the livestock needed feeding, and ice needed to be chipped to allow water to be fetched into the house. The fires were stoked, and Mary, now well on her way to giving birth to a second Parker child, was making breakfast. There is an indication that by this time, Captain Ebenezer Parker had removed to Standish to live with his son Eleazer and his wife Elizabeth and their children. Ebenezer and Mary, along with little Nathaniel, now probably occupied the home. Shortly after breakfast Ebenezer likely outfitted his horse and wagon, while Mary brought out a packed lunch and put it under the wagon seat. With his family settled in for the day, Deputy Parker kissed Mary and stepped up onto the wagon. Mary said goodbye to her husband, as he left for work, and then she stepped back into the warmer confides of the Parker home. Deputy Parker then likely pointed his horse in a westerly direction and headed to Saccarappa. Deputy Parker now held within his pocket another reason to again find Levi Quinby.

Chapter Four

A stock lithographic depiction of an early American blacksmith at work.
Image courtesy of the Library of Congress.

Joseph Drew

The life of Blacksmith Joseph Drew was far from the life described in Henry Wadsworth Longfellow's "Village Blacksmith," though some similarities may have existed. Even by his own admission, Joseph Drew was a bad seed. He had a rough start to life and it never got any better, or any easier. Joseph Drew was born in Shapleigh, at York County, on October 9th of 1783. He was raised in a Baptist home and he received a basic education. By the age of eighteen, in 1801, Drew moved to the York County town of Limerick and entered into an apprenticeship with an elder and established tradesman, a respected blacksmith named Abijah Felch.

Felch had come from Middlesex Massachusetts and he served in the revolution. He relocated to Limerick with his wife and their nine children, and it was there that he pursued his trade. And, it is in Limerick that Felch trained Joseph Drew in the hot-iron art of blacksmithing.

When Drew's apprenticeship ended, just before 1804, Drew left Limerick and moved back to his hometown of Shapleigh. He setup his own shop and set his hand to the trade of blacksmith. Yet, his impatience and his desire for more adventurous evenings appear to have gotten the best of him. Finding little profitable work, and even less night-time entertainment, Drew began to pay less and less attention to his business at Shapleigh. Soon Drew's blacksmith shop had completely failed. By 1805, Drew had sought out a new position in a place that would afford him more profitable days and more entertaining nights. Joseph Drew soon packed up his tools and belongings and moved to Saccarappa, where he found gainful employment working for Daniel Conant in his blacksmith shop on Main Street.

At Saccarappa, Drew found a social life that included drinking, gambling, swearing, fighting, and carousing of all sorts. It was a nightlife more fitting to his personality and Saccarappa was perfectly located from Falmouth Neck, where even more similar endeavors could be had. Though a devout church-going community was certainly in place throughout the area, it little bothered Joseph Drew. By his own admission, he had "little time for God." And, it appears that Drew was able to find several other like-minded cronies to spend his free time consorting with. And, in Falmouth Neck, many sailors and seamen would come in from the sea to lubricate their salty moods with sweet spirits. There, whenever Drew found himself in need of a more physically altercating way of entertaining himself, was usually able to find willing participants.

By the time the Embargo of 1806 had taken hold, there were many men who had little else to do but partake in such time-wasting activities as drinking, fighting, and gambling. And, since there was a plethora of excess frustration and anger to be found, Joseph Drew was able to find many willing accomplices to his favorite activity of fighting. By his own admission, he was a young man of considerable strength and passion. He was quick to anger and slow to cool. Drew was a man who enjoyed a good fight, and he was happy to take up anyone's cause, at any time, and exercise his own demons by delivering his own physical force and self-administered justice. He took pleasure in being a champion of the downtrodden, a defender of the abused, and a protector of the weak. This self-accepted altruistic rationalization of his unacceptable behavior allowed Joseph Drew many opportunities to vent his rage with little regret or acceptance of personal responsibility. It would prove to be his undoing.

When Levi Quinby and Drew began to work together, Quinby had found a friend in the likes of Joseph Drew. The two men were the same age, and both were employed at Conant's blacksmith shop. And, it appears both of these young men enjoyed the more rowdy night life and seedy social exchanges found in Saccarappa, and at the rough and tumble places of the Old Port, on Falmouth

Neck, where many of the grittier taverns catered to other like-minded sorts. Falmouth was also the place to go if a man wanted to find the company of loose women who made their living in the pursuit of entertaining men with a few extra schillings to spare. Falmouth Neck, aside from the many taverns and rum joints, had a few whorehouses located in the Old Port. Without any doubt, Saccarappa and the Falmouth area were exactly where Joseph Drew wanted to be, and where he found his new home.

Like Levi Quinby, Joseph Drew also had his problems with debt. On March 21st of 1806, Joseph was a co-defendant – along with William Webb Jr., - in a case in the Court of Common Pleas. Both men were sued by Daniel Gammon of Gorham for $14.95 plus court costs of $6.76 for damages. Gammon won his case and nothing more is seen of the matter. Yet, Josiah Gould's case against Levi Quinby seemed to have no end in sight. When Richard King allowed Levi Quinby to go free, presumably to have time to settle his debt with Gould, it appears Quinby did very little to make good use of the time he was given.

On the morning of Monday, January 11th of 1808, word had reached Levi Quinby that Deputy Ebenezer Parker was once again looking for him. But, this time, Levi Quinby had no plans of being arrested. Quinby took to carrying a club underneath his coat, and he had made comments that he would not be taken by Parker. Since Quinby also worked in the family mills, just across the street from the blacksmith shop, Quinby chose to hide away at the mill. But,

Parker had arrived in Saccarappa and his search for Levi Quinby had begun.

Chapter Five

The Saccarappa Blacksmith Shop as it appeared at the turn of the 20th century.
Photo courtesy of the Westbrook Historical Society.

With Malice, Aforethought.

Although it appears that Deputy Ebenezer Parker had been looking for Levi Quinby ever since Richard King had released him, Levi had been given a full two weeks to settle his legal difficulties. If Quinby had settled his debt, by paying Josiah Gould what Quinby had owed him, then Parker would not have been in Saccarappa on the afternoon of Monday, January 11th in 1808, looking for him. But, Parker intended to give Quinby one last opportunity to pay-up. If Quinby should fail to do so, then Parker was by duty obligated to once again locate and arrest Levi Quinby.

60.

Word had reached Quinby that Parker was in town and was actively looking for him. The rumor was that Parker had come to Saccarappa to arrest Quinby and deliver him to the Cumberland County Jail. But, Levi Quinby had no intentions of paying-up or being taken to jail. He was now carrying a wooden club under his coat and he was ducking in and out of doorways as he made his way through town, finally arriving at the family-owned mill located upon the Presumpscot Falls. But, Deputy Parker had received word that Quinby was at the mill and when Parker arrived at the falls Quinby hastily exited the mill through the back and ran for cover. Directly across the street from the mill on the falls was Daniel Conant's home and Quinby had the intention of lurking his way there. Conant was at the very least a part owner in both the mill and the blacksmith shop and he was Quinby's employer. Quinby entered Conant's house, but Conant wasn't home. Levi quickly grabbed-up a bottle of rum, and then exited through the back door, and made his way over to the blacksmith shop, where he worked part-time with Joseph Drew. Within moments, Quinby had made his way into the blacksmith shop where Joseph Drew was already hard at work, hammering-out lava-hot iron into straight-cut nails.

No doubt, Drew could tell that Levi was upset and Quinby told Drew of his predicament with the deputy and that Parker was coming. Quinby was pulling gulps of liquor from the bottle he stole from his employer's home and he was pacing back and forth like a cornered rat, as he worried and menaced aloud. Quinby then closed the shop doors and locked them as best as he could. Quinby then pulled the cork and took another swig from the rum bottle. Quinby was in a fit of anxiousness and his mouth ran amok foretelling the troubles he would give Parker should the Deputy find him. Meanwhile, Parker had received word that Quinby was hiding away in the shop and that he was armed with a club and had no intention of being arrested. Parker was then joined by Samuel Cox, a few other men, and Richard King, the man who agreed to allow Quinby to go free just two weeks before. It was "Old Dick" King that Quinby gave his word to, that he would surrender if asked to do so, and Parker hoped Quinby would keep his word.

The former Conant's Blacksmith Shop can be seen in the middle of this image, between Waterhouse Clothier's Shop on the left, and Day's Carriage Shop on the far right. Image courtesy of the Westbrook Historical Society.

By the evening hours, Quinby was still locked away in the blacksmith shop with Drew, and Parker sought a reasonable outcome to the situation. He located William Babb Jr., a friend of both Drew and Quinby and sent him into the shop to speak with the excitable

Levi. Quinby allowed Babb to enter the shop, where the men talked. Babb told him Parker wanted Levi to settle the debt, as ordered by the court. And, Babb had already talked with Daniel Conant, Quinby's employer, who offered to settle the debt with Parker if Levi would agree to the solution. But, Quinby refused the offer. Babb told him Parker had a posse of men with him and meant business. Babb pleaded with Quinby to allow Conant to settle the matter, but Quinby refused to give his necessary consent. Babb then told Parker of the outcome of the discussion and returned to the shop. Parker had no options left for a reasonable solution to the standoff. It was cold, the dark of the evening had already settled over Saccarappa, and the law had to be executed. And, with Quinby's refusal to settle the matter, Deputy Parker and his men approached the blacksmith shop and knocked on the door.

Levi Quinby stepped back and stood by the red-hot forge with a club in his hand. Quinby suddenly got very quiet and had nothing to say, but Joseph Drew stepped away from the red-hot forge and approached the door. "Who is there?" asked Drew. "Parker" stated the deputy. "Are you well?" asked Drew. "Yes, I am," answered the county lawman. "Then I advise you to stay where you are," Drew replied. "I do not want you," Parker told him, "I am here for Quinby." More words were bandied about between the blacksmith and the deputy and Drew was beginning to grow angry with each word uttered. Parker realized he had a standoff on his hands and realized a forced action was his only remaining option. Parker called out to Quinby to step out of the shop, but Quinby remained still and silent. Drew then responded to Parker that he should keep out.

Deputy Parker then reached under the door and pulled it outward, as the latch gave way and opened. Drew immediately threw down the nail rod he had been working on and picked up a sledge hammer. Drew's anger now rose to a full-throttled rage as he stepped out of the shop onto the outdoor walkway. "What are you breaking open my shop for?" Drew demanded as he continued, "stand  by or I will throw this sledge through you! Drew then swung at an unarmed Parker, who ducked behind the shop door. Drew then pulled back and swung again, this time at Old Dick King, but again missed. Drew then threw the sledge through the air at King and struck him in the chest. But, the blow was only a glancing one and King was relatively unhurt.

When Quinby, still hidden inside the shop, saw Drew's hand was empty Quinby threw the club he had been holding outward, through the doorway, to the ground at Drew's feet. Drew picked up the club just as Parker stepped out from behind the door. When Drew saw Parker he pulled back the club with both hands and swung the club at the deputy. Parker jumped back and Drew's first swing missed and struck the door with such force that the door swung shut and slammed against the frame of the doorway. Drew then stepped

64.

forward as he swung the club again, this time striking Parker in the head. As Parker fell to the ground, with blood already gushing from his deep and gaping wound, Drew then swung the club again. The

third swing of the club struck the fallen Parker on the back of the shoulders, at the base of the neck. King rushed forward towards Drew who then swung the club and struck Old Dick, who then fell to the ground. Once again, King was not terribly hurt. The other men of the posse also tried to close ranks and rush Drew who swung the club wildly. Then, Drew looked down and saw the bloody and motionless Parker on the ground. Seeing the damage done, Drew then turned, opened the shop door, and walked back inside the blacksmith shop. Still holding the mortal weapon in his hand and seething with rage, he slammed the door shut behind him. When Drew saw William Babb still standing in the shop he commanded Babb to go out and remove Parker, "take up your dead lawman," Drew told Babb. Quinby had remained by the forge, nearly frozen in his tracks while his friend defended him against the law. His only move was to toss a club to his friend who then picked up the weapon and laid the lawman still and dying. Babb quickly stepped out of the shop to assist King and Cox and the other men to attend to the dying Deputy Parker.

Drew's rage was still not satisfied. In fact, his momentum was still seething and he commanded Quinby to secure the doors and windows, which Levi immediately did. Then Drew opened a window and began yelling to the crowds of onlookers who had just witnessed the brutal and nefarious events outside of Conant's Blacksmith

Shop. Drew yelled obscenities and threatened all who could hear, that they may bring on as many as had a mind to challenge him. He warned that each man would "have sore heads" should they try. Meanwhile, Babb, Cox, Old Dick King, and the other men had grabbed up Deputy Parker and ran for a nearby boarding house. They got Parker inside and tried to warm him and control the bleeding. They could tell that Parker was in bad shape and they could not wait for a doctor to be summoned from Stroudwater. It is likely that Old Dick King then bundled up his wounded friend into a wagon and made a mad run for the nearest doctor to save time. Meanwhile, Samuel Cox and the other men – still deputized – had a duty to take Drew and Quinby into custody.

The cold evening hours were turning into early night as the frosty January temperatures were dropping. Old Dick King was rushing his horse onward, as fast as he could coax the animal to run.

66.

Doctor Jeremiah Barker's office was located at his home in Stroudwater, about three miles away, and King could only pray that Barker would be home and not off on another medical case somewhere in the area. When King arrived at Barker's office, near the Stroudwater Falls, - given the time of night - he likely found Barker at home. Barker most likely examined Parker out in the wagon and saw the gash in Parker's head. The wound was four inches long and three inches wide. Worst yet, the gaping wound was also two inches deep and his skull was seriously fractured and bleeding profusely. Barker, a country doctor, knew the extent of the wound was out of his league. He likely applied a bandage and

advised King to take Parker to the only doctor he knew of that could possibly help the stricken deputy. Moments later, King was thrashing the horses as fast as they would run, eastward, along the road to Falmouth Neck.

Jeremiah Barker had undoubtedly sent King onward to Falmouth Neck to see Dr. Nathaniel Coffin Jr. Coffin was an eminent surgeon who specialized in trephining of head wounds, and Barker knew that the deputy would need just the kind of specialized care that only Coffin could give. But, Coffin's office was located at the corner of Middle Street and King Street (Now India Street) on the Peninsula of Falmouth Neck. Coffin's home was another five miles distant and at least another thirty to forty-minute ride. For as miserable as the cold temperature was it now served as an asset to both King and especially to Parker. The cold would help to slow Deputy Parker's bleeding, which could buy time as King whipped the horse along the road to Falmouth Neck, over the hill of Congress Street, and toward the base of Munjoy's Hill. Once again, old Dick King could only pray, this time that Doctor Nathaniel Coffin Jr., would be home.

Chapter Six

Sketch of Dr. Nathaniel Coffin Jrs', Home & Office, located at what was once King Street in Falmouth Neck. The location is now 35 India Street, in Portland Maine. Sketch by Charles Quincy Goodhue, 1902.

Cold Nights, Painful Days.

In Saccarappa, Samuel Cox and the men who were with Deputy Parker were busy trying to dislodge Joseph Drew and Levi Quinby from Daniel Conant's Blacksmith Shop. Drew had raged on with threats and continued a fury-laden posturing, as he dared locals and deputies, with threats to deliver "sore heads" upon any who dared to enter the shop. Levi Quinby, the man whose own debts, and bad choices, had caused the entire day's horrible events, had remained in the shop, frozen – some say – with fear, while his friend took up his defense. Some witnesses reported that Quinby cowered in a corner, but official statements say he never stepped away from the blacksmith's forge. But, he did toss the fateful weapon, which dispatched Parker, down at Drew's feet. Though not much is known about the eventual arrest of Joseph Drew, or Levi Quinby, both men were eventually arrested and taken to the Cumberland County Jail, which in 1808 was located at the rear of where the Portland City Hall now stands.

When old Dick King Arrived at Dr. Coffin's office, just a short distance from the jail, Dr. Coffin was home, and he quickly helped King to bring the limp and bloody deputy into his office. The oil lamps and candles were quickly lit and Dr. Coffin began a long evening of work on the mortal wounds of Deputy Ebenezer Parker.

Dr. Coffin also began a long effort to warm the nearly frozen deputy. Coffin found the extensive wounds to Parker's head were wide, long, and deep. The skull was fractured and swelling of the brain had undoubtedly occurred. A great deal of blood had been lost but had also built up within the head wound  itself, under the skull. As Dr. Barker has suspected, Parker would need a surgical technique known as trephining. This procedure is where a hole is bored into the skull to relieve pressure and drain blood, and Dr. Coffin was known as the best in the area when it came to this technique. The surgeon set out his instruments and got to work.

When Coffin had finished, Parker was allowed to rest. He had not regained consciousness but he had survived the procedure and there were indications that he could survive the ordeal. By now, Parker was likely transferred to his home for round-the-clock care by his family. Dr. Coffin was not known for caring for patients at his home, but was known for traveling – from town to town – to care for his patients, even the critical ones, in their own homes. By now, Ebenezer's mother, who lived nearby, and his youngest sister Deborah had probably joined Mary in caring for Ebenezer. Doubtless, Sheriff Waite, deputies, and other nearby Parkers, had also arrived at the house to give whatever help or support they could. Word was likely sent out to Ebenezer's sisters at Gorham, Standish, and Durham, who likely came as soon as they received word. This was a tight, close-knit family, and it is probable the Parker home at Cape Elizabeth was soon full of family helping to see to Mary and Ebenezer. And, it is also likely that Dr. Coffin was making daily visits to check on Ebenezer.

For both Joseph Drew and Levi Quinby, they too were receiving visitors. Local ministers were making their rounds within the community and the Cumberland County Jail was one of their daily stops, much as it still is today. The Reverends Samuel Deane, Caleb Bradley, and Thomas Smith, all found particular interest in turning incarcerated inmates into saved souls, and Levi Quinby and Joseph Drew were both of particular interest to the ministers. Quinby and Drew were two examples of sinful wickedness, which these ministers could each exploit as prime, living examples of why each common man and woman must turn from sin and come to God, through the church. And, it is said, that no minister did this better than Caleb Bradley. And, Bradley himself took a particular interest in Joseph Drew.

Both Quinby and Drew, along with a few other inmates, were being kept in the lower holding area cells of the jail. In these stone-walled and dungeon-like cells, Drew and Quinby awaited their fate. Quinby, among other matters, still had a debt to Josiah Gould to answer for. For Drew, at best, he was facing assault charges. However, should Deputy Parker not survive Drew would surely face a charge of murder or manslaughter. Either way, neither Drew nor Quinby would be going anywhere until the whole mess of what took place in Saccarappa was sorted out by officials, and while the well-being of Deputy Parker was still being determined.

By late Wednesday, word of the events at Saccarappa had spread through Cumberland County like wildfire. The epic story of Drew striking down a debt-seeking lawman had delivered a much-desired heroic Gideon-like savior to all of the beleaguered souls of an economic depression that had sorely tested and afflicted every man, woman, and child in Cumberland County. With every retelling of the story, a new detail or twist was added to the tale. By late Wednesday night, Drew's fight with the Sheriff's Posse and his assault on Deputy Parker had taken on an air of epic and heroic legend. The facts were twisted. Truths were stretched to the breaking point. Deputy Ebenezer Parker was instantly vilified, while Joseph Drew was mythically lionized. A new tale of the common man who had literally struck back at the system and laid cold the evil debt collector, spread from house to house, tavern to tavern, and street corner to street corner. By Thursday, January 14th, the name Joseph Drew was on the lips of nearly every man in Falmouth and the tale was still being told again and again, with new rumors added and facts eliminated. There was no stopping the rumor mill or the rapid word-of-mouth re-telling of the events that had become welcome news to the wanting ears of many who were now homeless, hungry, out of work, and destitute, in Cumberland County.

While Deputy Parker continued to linger, and Dr. Coffin continued to drain and bandage Parker's wounds, only prayers, and patience could help the Parker family as they did all they could for their fallen husband, father, brother, and family guardian and provider. By Saturday, January 16th, Parker had thus far lasted six days, and there was hope he might pull through. Yet, the reality wasn't good. The blow delivered to Parker by Joseph Drew was indeed considered to be a mortal or fatal wound. It was a miracle that Ebenezer had survived this long. But, with each passing day, it was hoped that he would heal more, gain strength, and survive. However, Parker had not yet regained consciousness, and that undoubtedly concerned Dr. Coffin, as well as the rest of the Parker clan.

Meanwhile, the local newspapers had spent much of the week gathering the story and details of the events at Saccarappa on January 11th, and typesetters had spent much of their time – as they did each week – setting the typeset and preparing the newspapers for the new editions, which generally took a great deal of time. Most of the editions of the newspapers from 1806 to 1809 are filled, for each of the first two pages, with word on the Embargo, the war in Europe, and the economic woes of the nation and the area. And, at least one or more pages are filled with legal and commercial – revenue-generating – advertisements and notices. What was left, as far as available column space, was given to the most important "other" news of the day. And, with most of these papers seemingly limited to four pages, not much space was given to stories that everyone had already heard about. The Portland Gazette published each Monday and did not see fit to report on the assault at all in their next edition to go out after the assault occurred.

However, the Eastern Argus, which was a major publication that was also published in Portland, was published every Thursday. And, the Eastern Argus did cover a brief story of the report of the assault at Saccarappa, which appeared on the third page of their January

Unfortunate Occurrence.

On Monday evening last, at Sacarappa, in Falmouth, Mr. Ebenezer Parker, a Deputy-Sheriff, of Cape Elizabeth, in attempting to apprehend a Mr. Quinby, was violently assaulted with a club by one Joseph Drew; Mr. Parker received a number of blows on the head, which fractured his skull, and his life is despaired of. Drew has since been apprehended, and after an examination before S. Freeman, Esq. was committed to jail, for trial at the Supreme Court in May next.

14th edition of the Eastern Argus. The article was titled, "An Unfortunate Occurrence." Whether the Freeman's Friend or Eastern Argus had planned to cover the entire story in more detail, in their next editions, is something we may never know.

On Sunday morning, January 17th, at about seven in the morning – while many were getting ready for early morning worship services – fire alarms began ringing throughout Falmouth Neck. A fire had been discovered in the Haymarket Row buildings, located on Middle Street near the present-day Monument Square. The ground was covered in freshly fallen snow and temperatures were bitterly cold. When the alarms rang out men sprang to their horses and carriages and rushed to help. Alarm bells then echoed through the peninsula and reached outward into Stroudwater, where Reverend Caleb Bradley was preparing for Sunday morning services at both his Stroudwater Parish and the Cape Elizabeth Parish. Bradley quickly rushed to Falmouth Neck and helped fight the fires until late in the evening.

Hay Market Row was a long stretch of three-story buildings which all housed about eight different stores and several smaller offices, including a wholesale company, a cabinet maker, a book publisher and printing shop, and two newspapers; The Freeman's Friend and the Eastern Argus. The fire had devastated the row of buildings and burned into the late evening before being contained and fully extinguished. The businesses were completely, or to some degree, all badly damaged. With great effort expended, the Eastern Argus was able to save its equipment, though its typeset for the next edition had been completely wrecked. The Argus was able to move to another building and reorganize quickly but was not able to publish a full

Eastern Argus.

PORTLAND :
THURSDAY, JANUARY 21, 1808.

Diftreffing Fire !

ON Sunday morning laft, about 10 minutes before 8 o'clock, the citizens of this town were alarmed by the diftreffing cry of Fire ; which proved to be in *Hay-Market-Row*, a range of new brick buildings in Middle-ftreet. The fire was firft difcovered by the fmoke burfting from the windows of the fecond and third ftory of Store No. 4 ; the firft and fecond floors of which were unoccupied ; the third was improved by Mr. Wm. Weeks, publifher of the "Freeman's Friend ;" & the fourth by T. B. Wait & Co. as a ftore-room for paper. The printing materials of Mr. Weeks, together with his books and papers, were totally loft. The fire immediately communicated to Store No. 3 ; the firft and

75.

edition that week. In fact, they normally published four pages for each edition, but the next edition of the Eastern Argus, on January 21st, was only a two-page edition.

The day after the fire, Monday, January 18th of 1808, was a day of cold and pain for many at Falmouth Neck. While the owners and occupants of Hay Market Row were sifting through the still-smoldering ashes of their businesses, the Parkers, and Dr. Coffin, were continuing to attend to Ebenezer Parker at Cape Elizabeth. Once again, Dr. Coffin had to drain Parker's head wound and change the bloody bandages. Mary, Ebenezer's mother Hannah, and Ebenezer's seven sisters had held vigil over him all week. These women had cleaned him, changed his sheets, and done all they could to keep him warm, comfortable, hydrated, and nourished. By late in the afternoon Ebenezer seemed to be regaining consciousness and the family had felt all their prayers were being answered. Dr. Coffin could have only felt it was a good and encouraging sign that indicated Parker might just survive, after all. But, Coffin also knew there was still a long and perilous road ahead of the deputy and the future prognosis for his badly damaged patient was still murky, at best.

Suddenly, Ebenezer opened his eyes for the first time since the brutal assault had occurred a week earlier. He looked around at his surroundings and saw the faces of his family. He called out for his wife and his two-year-old son Nathaniel, and he then turned his gaze upon his bride and his son as each sat on the bed next to him. After a few minutes with them, and after a few words they may have

76.

shared, Deputy Ebenezer Parker slowly closed his eyes and his life slipped away. He was just forty-four years of age.

The Last Moments Of Deputy Ebenezer Parker

> Parker in an unconscious condition, was taken to a neighboring hotel and surgical aid was summoned. He was unconscious many days. About the seventh day, the skull was trephined by surgeons from Portland. Soon after the trephining, Parker regained consciousness, recognized his wife and called for the baby, which was brought to him.

A portion of the story as it appeared in the Bridgton News, September 11, 1903.

For the Parkers of Cape Elizabeth, a family guardian, and provider had been lost. Ebenezer Parker had lived a life of adventure and responsibility. From serving a fledgling nation under attack to providing for a family of widows, young ladies, and orphans, to serving his County as a deputy in the Cumberland County Sheriff's Office, Deputy Parker was a man whom his family and his community had relied upon, looked up to, and needed. Now the Parker family had lost all three of its men, from family patriarch Nathaniel to his son John, and now Ebenezer. As for Mary, she had now lost her husband and the father of her first born son, Nathaniel. Mary was now a widow, and Ebenezer's second child – due at any time – would never get to know his father. Now, Mary had no protector or provider for her or her children. Their future, one which just a week before had seemed so settled, was now as unsettled and as uncertain as anything Mary could imagine.

As for Joseph Drew and Levi Quinby, the death of Deputy Parker also brought uncertainty for their futures as well. Undoubtedly, word quickly reached the Sheriff's Office that Sheriff Waite's languishing deputy had finally succumbed to his injuries, and thus word likely spread rapidly to the jail as well. Most likely, Joseph M. Gerrish, a Cumberland County Deputy Sheriff, and Cumberland County Keeper of the Jail had delivered the news to Joseph Drew and Levi Quinby. If either of these two men had any ideas they might soon be released from jail, word of Parkers death surely would have quashed those hopes. There could be no doubt that both Quinby and Drew would likely remain in jail for some time, as they awaited word of what charges they may face, and then even longer as they both awaited arraignment, indictment, and trial. All they could do now was sit, wait, and pray for leniency.

Chapter Seven

Reverend Caleb Bradley. Photo courtesy of the Westbrook Historical Society.

Just The beginning

On Wednesday, January 20th of 1808, for the second time in three weeks, the Parker family prepared themselves for another family funeral at Cape Elizabeth. Just three weeks before, the family had buried Captain Ebenezer Parker's wife, Esther Higgins Parker. Now, the family gathered to say good bye to the younger Deputy Ebenezer Parker. Since his passing two days before, the family had held his wake in the Parker home. Undoubtedly, Parkers from all over Cumberland County had arrived to pay their respects. And, it is most probable that there was a contingent of Cumberland County

Deputies also in the house as would have been John Waite, the High Sheriff himself. The family had lost a son, a brother, a father, a husband, and a provider. And, the County had lost a good man, a deputy, who had served his community in times of war and peace. Now, everyone gathered to say their good-byes.

Ebenezer Parker's Death Notice.

At Saccarappa (Falmouth) Mr. *Ebenezer Parker* of Cape-Elizabeth, a deputy Sheriff, in consequence of blows received upon his head from one Joseph Drew. Parker, the preceeding day to that on which the assault was committed, arrested a Mr. Quinby and left him with a keeper from whom he escaped to Drew's shop, who is a blacksmith. Parker on going to the shop to take him again was forbid entering ; a man in company however pushed the door open, at whom Drew threw a sledge and then took up a piece of a sleigh arm and with the first blow felled P. to the ground and repeated the blows several times, his skull was fractured in a shocking manner, he languished several days. Drew has been committed to jail in this town, to take his trial for murder at the Supreme Judicial Court in May next.

As it appeared in the Freeman's Friend. January 25, 1808.

In those times, it usually fell to the men of the family to dig the graves of the dead in the family or local cemeteries. However, in the Parker family, few young men of age-enough to take on such a hard winter's labor were left. Of the original Parker settlers at Cape Elizabeth, Joseph, and Elisha had both died years before and their

80.

children were now past their middle ages. Elisha's sons had left Cape Elizabeth and removed eastward and began a shipbuilding business in the Washington and Penobscot County areas. Many of Joseph's grandchildren were scattered along the coastal area and the sons of Ebenezer's sisters were still too young for the harsh duty of frozen ground-digging. It is likely that either Ebenezer's fellow Cumberland County Deputies personally dug his grave, or the Sheriff had hired a few of the many unemployed locals for the gruesome task. Either way, though many might think Ebenezer was held over for a spring burial there is suggestive evidence that he was buried two days after his death.

It also fell to a male family member to build a coffin for their dearly departed. In those early American days, there were few actual coffin makers in the District of Maine, and since most men had carpentry skills, they simply made their own. It is likely that one of Deputy Parker's brothers-in-law built the coffin in which Ebenezer would now spend eternity. Deputy Parker's youngest sister Deborah had married to Isaac Junkins – a shipwright – who lived just across the harbor in Falmouth Neck. The task of building a coffin for Ebenezer probably fell to Isaac to complete, as he would have been close, and had the tools, and the knowledge, to do so. And, being that Ebenezer's prognosis was doubtful all along, Isaac may have already had the materials for the coffin gathered and at the ready.

In 1808, there were no funeral homes, nor was there any embalming. Once a person had died, some families – dependent on religious beliefs – may have stopped the clocks in the house and may have covered the mirrors. The women cleaned and dressed the body as the deceased was usually laid out in bed, as if asleep. During winter, the windows in the bedroom, where the deceased was laid to rest, were kept open regardless of the outdoor temperature to allow the miasma of decay to escape and to allow the body to remain chilled by the cold air. A minister would arrive and lead the family in prayer. Visitors and family members would come by throughout the day and into the evening to say their goodbyes. This wake took place the day after Ebenezer's death had occurred, and the funeral took place the very next day.

Deputy Parker's Funeral was likely not the sort of funeral we know today for a fallen hero. When Deputy Ebenezer Parker died from his wounds, suffered in the line of duty, he became the first fallen law enforcement officer to die in the line of duty in New England history.

Jan. 20. Attended the funeral of Parker who was killed by Drew at Saccarappa.

Reverend Caleb Bradley's diary entry on the funeral of Ebenezer Parker, as it appears in Leonard Bond Chapman's book, "Grandpa's Scrapbook."

And, it is doubtful that any sort of official honors had yet been designed to honor such a sacrifice. And, with the local antagonism created by both the Embargo and by Joseph Drew and his mythical legend, any sort of plans for an official funeral might have been kept low-key or not carried out at all. Either way, it is doubtful that Deputy Ebenezer Parker had received much posthumous acknowledgment of his duty or his historic sacrifice. Instead, it is

82.

most likely that his funeral was kept low-key, as was the way of the times, and kept within the moral and spiritual traditions of the

 family's faith, and respectfully guided by the wishes of the family.

On Wednesday, January 20th, Reverend Caleb Bradley left his parish in Stroudwater and made the trek to Cape Elizabeth to attend to the funeral of Ebenezer Parker. It is likely that after prayers were held at the family home, Cumberland County Deputies – led by Sheriff Waite – would have carried their brother-in-justice, their Fallen Star, upon their shoulders to the graveyard on Meeting House Hill, while the Parker family, friends, and others, walked in a procession behind the coffin.

Once at the cemetery, the deputies would have eased Deputy Parker's coffin down into his eternal resting place, in a long-lot where his grandfather Joseph, and his grandmother Prudence, as well as his father Nathaniel, and great Uncle Elisha, were all laid to eternal rest. And, he was likely laid to rest alongside the woman that Deputy Parker himself had just helped to bury only three weeks earlier, Esther Higgins Parker. After the services were concluded at the graveside, it is likely that either the deputies or men hired for the job, filled in the grave and buried Deputy Ebenezer Parker.

While Deputy Parker's funeral service was being held, in the shadow of the church his grandfather and great uncle had built, at

Cape Elizabeth, the futures of Levi Quinby and Joseph Drew were being planned out at Falmouth

Neck. Both men were charged in the death of Deputy Parker, and the Commonwealth of Massachusetts had decided to try Drew and Quinby separately in Parker's death. Both defendants now had their trials set for the upcoming

spring session of the Supreme Judicial Court at Falmouth Neck.

Massachusetts Solicitor General Daniel Davis was set to prosecute the case. Davis had come to Maine in about 1782, from Boston, and was appointed in 1796 by President George Washington to serve as the United States attorney for the District of Maine. Davis resided on Congress Street, just a few doors down from the County Jail and Courthouse, and since his position changed in 1801 when Davis became the Solicitor General of Massachusetts, the trial fell under his authority.

For Joseph Drew, two attorneys - Nicholas Emery and John Holmes - were appointed to represent him on the charge of murder. Nicholas Emery was a thirty-two-year-old, New Hampshire-born graduate of Dartmouth Academy. And, he had only been an attorney for about ten years when he moved to Falmouth Neck, in 1807.

Defense Team For Joseph Drew.

John Holmes (Left). Nicholas Emery (Right).
Courtesy of the Maine Historical Society.

Now, Emery was appointed to defend this high-profile
capital murder case. As for John Holmes, he was a thirty-five-year-
old, Kingston Massachusetts-born graduate of what is now Brown
University. Holmes was admitted to the Bar in 1799 and had been
practicing law for even less time than Emery. Holmes was more of a
sarcastic and temperamental politician who had served in the
Massachusetts State Legislature in 1802, and 1803. He lived in
Alfred, at York County, yet he was now chosen to second-chair the
defense of Joseph Drew at Falmouth Neck.

Levi Quinby would be represented, at his own request, by the
court-appointed Prentiss Mellen and Stephen Longfellow, Jr. Mellen
was a forty-four-year-old, Sterling Massachusetts born, Harvard
graduate who was perhaps the more experienced of the two attorneys
as he was admitted to the Bar in 1788. He had moved to Falmouth
Neck in 1806 after a brief residency in Biddeford. Mellen's second-
chair defense attorney, representing Levi Quinby, was Stephen

Longfellow Jr., of Gorham, Maine. Longfellow was just thirty-two years old and a 1798 graduate of Harvard University.

Defense Team For Levi Quinby

Prentiss Mellen (Left), and Stephen Longfellow (Right).
Courtesy of the Maine Historical Society.

Longfellow was admitted to the Bar in 1801. One of his young law clerks, in the Longfellow Office, as it turns out, was Levi Quinby's first cousin – Moses Quinby. Longfellow was the son of the Gorham Town Selectman Stephen Longfellow, the man who had ordered the widow of John Parker – her children and her mother - to leave Gorham in 1790. Now, Longfellow's son was defending one of the men accused of murdering the man who spoiled his father's plans, nearly twenty years before.

For Daniel Davis, it appeared his case against Drew was air tight. There were a number of witnesses who were ready to testify and there was little doubt, held by anyone, that Drew was guilty of the assault. The only question appeared to be whether Drew would be convicted of murder or manslaughter. As for Davis' case against

Quinby, Davis felt his case was strong in prosecuting a charge of aiding and abetting the murder. But, again, the question remained, was it aiding and abetting in murder or manslaughter?

An artist's rendering of Congress Street in about 1800 shows the homes of Daniel Davis (Left), Reverend Samuel Deane (Center), and the 1st Parish Church (Right).

The decision was quickly made to prosecute the case against Drew first, see which charge would win the case, and then try Quinby for that charge. But, before either the prosecution or the defense could begin to try the cases, they first had to pick the twelve men for each jury. Many of the most upstanding men in the area were chosen for this civic duty.

Many of the surnames of these jurors are names that are still recognizable today to the inhabitants of modern-day Portland. For the trial of Joseph Drew James Merrill was chosen as the foreman, and James Curtis Jr., Eben Collins, James Doughty, Jonathan Philbrick, Isaiah Ingalls, Job Randall, Stephen Tukey, William Cutter, Joseph Pride, Thomas Freeman, and John Lord rounded out the chosen twelve. For Levi Quinby's trial, the foreman was John

Lincoln, Jonathan Moulton 3rd, Seth Carpenter, Aaron Snow, David Free, John Milliken, Thomas Beck, Richard Codman, Ichabod Hanson Jr., Peter White, Thomas Cross, and James Phinney Jr., were all sworn in to serve the Commonwealth.

Both Quinby and Drew had each been arraigned, each pleaded not guilty, and both were charged: Drew with Murder; Quinby with aiding and abetting Joseph Drew in committing murder. Both Joseph Drew and Levi Quinby were then returned to jail to await trial. Each man had just over four months to sit, reflect, and await their fate.

Chapter Eight

The four official trial summary pages for the trials of both Quinby and Drew.
Courtesy Maine State Library Archives.

The Trial of Joseph Drew

By May 26th of 1808, Mary Parker had somewhere to be.
She now had two little boys to care for, having given birth to
Ebenezer's second son sometime after his death, and it is likely that
she was also caring for an elderly Captain Ebenezer Parker, a
widower since the death of his wife Esther three weeks before the
murder of Mary's husband. Although she had a lot to do in Cape
Elizabeth, she would not miss this day at Falmouth Neck. And, she
had the escort of a man who had come to be of great help to her and
her children since her husband's passing.

The Reverend Caleb Bradley was still covering the Cape Elizabeth Congregational Church on Meeting House Hill, while the search was on to hire a more permanent and dedicated full-time minister. Bradley had taken a great interest in the welfare of Mary and her two sons. Bradley was likely very influential and helpful to her in her time of need, as she likely named her newly born son Caleb after the man American Poet Nathaniel Hawthorne would later describe as an old curmudgeon. And, aside from his interest in Mary Parker, Bradley was also quite interested in the life of Joseph Drew.

May 24—Supreme court sets today. Attended Drew and Quinby who were indicted for murder.

Rev. Bradley's diary entry as it was transcribed by Leonard Bond Chapman, and appeared in Chapman's book *"Grandpa's Scrapbook."*

He had been visiting Drew regularly at the jail and working to convince Drew to repent for his life of sin and wickedness. Now, as the trial of Joseph Drew was about to begin, the Reverend Bradley escorted the Widow Parker into the Courtroom on Congress Street. Her presence in the courtroom would be an important piece of sympathetic theatrics for the prosecution to put on before the jury, as the widow sat there with a toddler in tow and an infant at her bosom.

Outside of the courthouse crowds of men and women with great interest in the case of Joseph Drew had begun gathering. Inside the small courtroom, a commotion of voices and curiosities abounded as the Commonwealth's Prosecutor and Drew's two defense attorneys prepared their tables with papers, affidavits, and documents. When Chief Justice Parsons and Associate Justice Sewell and Associate Justice Thatcher entered the courtroom, everyone finally settled down. Soon, as Mary Parker – seated next to Reverend Bradley - looked on, the court was called to order. Then, the side door opened and a rattle of chains could be heard. Two deputies, with drawn swords, entered the courtroom. Behind these men came Joseph Drew, followed by two more armed deputies. Drew's legs were shackled by chains to his waist, where a chain belt then bound his cuffed hands to his torso, and another chain stretched from his waist upward to a steel collar around Drew's neck. Drew shuffled into the courtroom and was escorted to a seat that was set alone in the middle of the room, before the justices, and between the prosecution and defense tables. All who were in the room were commanded to stand as the jury of twelve men entered the room to take their seats in the jury stand. The room was packed from wall to wall with little room to move, except before the bench where the attorneys would work.

It was immediately evident to officials that there was a problem. The case of Joseph Drew had created so much attention with the public, and with the press, that demands for a larger public venue for the trial was being demanded. However, the courtroom was a small one and could not accommodate any more of an audience than had already been seated. Yet, outside the courthouse, large crowds had gathered and were growing as more and more people were arriving each hour for up-to-the-minute word on the wellbeing of their Gideon, Joseph Drew. The justices, the attorneys, and the Cumberland County Sheriff, John Waite, then decided to move the trial just down the road to Reverend Elijah Kellogg's Second Meeting House on Middle Street. There, the larger venue could indeed accommodate a greater audience. Chief Justice Parsons then announced the decision to the courtroom, dismissed the jury – pending a re-convening of the trial at the meeting house - and then he adjourned the case.

More deputies were brought in and each had drawn their swords as they en-circled Joseph Drew. The lawmen then stepped out of the courthouse as they escorted Joseph Drew for a public walk to the Meeting House, just a few thousand feet away. Although the deputies' swords were drawn, the deputies were not necessarily guarding against the possible escape of Joseph Drew. Although they were to insure Drew's arrival at his trial, the deputies had surrounded Drew to protect him from any ne'er-do-wells who might try retribution for Parkers murder. Although the public humiliation at such a walk in chains might seem formidable to face, Joseph Drew is believed to have enjoyed the walk. It had been the first time he had been outdoors since his being jailed in January. Now, with the late May warmth, and sun shining down on his face, Drew could only have enjoyed his walk to the Meeting House.

Crowds had lined both sides of Congress Street and Temple Street, from the Courthouse to the Meeting House, and many had yelled, jeered, laughed or cheered, cried, or just stared at the sight of Drew in chains as he shuffled to his trial.

The Second Meeting House

The Meeting House steeple is seen in the background from 1846.
Courtesy of the Maine Historical Society.

Every spectator most likely had some manner of comment to be made. Catcalls or whistles, rude comments or well wishes, much like today, it is likely that many comments were made either towards Joseph Drew or the deputies who escorted and protected him. There were no jobs to be at, nor other matters to draw their attention. The Murder Trial of Joseph Drew was an all-star event. People came from many towns away, and some even dressed as if they were going to church. Entire families packed a picnic basket and rode into town to spend the day and await the news of the trial. Some walked through the crowds selling homemade keepsakes to remember the day, and many local businesses closed up shop and carried their wares about the crowds as they hawked their goods on the hoof. Cold drinks were available, and so were slices of pie, cakes, and cookies, all home-baked and for sale by women hoping to make a few schillings. Young boys had found work earning a few pennies here and there. For a few who were quick on their feet, running into the Meeting House to hear what they could of the trial, then running out to their employer to inform him of all they had heard, had earned these industrious lads quick money throughout the day.

Inside the Meeting House, the trial was about to proceed. Drew had been given his place to be seated and the jury had been brought in. The gallery was filled with spectators of every age, though almost every one of these watchers were men. The attorneys were set and ready and the justices had been seated. Deputies were placed all around the meeting house to maintain the peace, both upstairs and down. Chief Justice Parsons began the court proceedings by delivering

instructions to the lawyers and the jury, as to the particulars of the case before them, and the legal protocols to be adhered to. Then, Justice Parsons called upon Samuel Freeman, the Clerk of the Court, to read the charges that the Commonwealth of Massachusetts had charged against Joseph Drew. The Clerk read that in fact, the charge was murder.

However, there was a serious debate as to what charges should be brought against Drew. It was immediately argued in the opening statement made by prosecutor Daniel Davis that Joseph Drew did "wantonly, and with malice aforethought, murder Deputy Ebenezer Parker." Yet, in the opening statement of the defense, they countered that the charge against Drew should not be murder, but

94.

manslaughter. Although it may seem a fine line to draw, the charge of manslaughter could carry from a certain amount of years incarcerated up to a term of life imprisoned at hard labor, decided at the discretion of the court. But, a conviction on the charge of murder could only result in the court ordering the defendant's execution by hanging.

It was surprisingly clear from the initial start of the trial that this case before the court would not be about the guilt or the innocence of the defendant, but about the penalty that defendant must pay for his crime. Even though Drew had pleaded "not guilty," it appeared that both the prosecution and the defense were each starting with an unstated stipulation that Joseph Drew was indeed guilty in the death of Deputy Ebenezer Parker. The trial would be more about haggling out the details of the charges to meet the criteria for the desired result each side of the case was seeking.

Daniel Davis was prepared to argue his case based on the murder of either a deputy - a law enforcement officer - or the extinguishment of a plain and ordinary citizen. Davis wanted to easily counter-argue a claim the defense was making that Deputy Parker had over-stepped his lawful authority as a deputy and therefore Drew had a right to defend his friend from an unauthorized arrest. Drew's attorneys, Nicholas Emery, and John Holmes argued that since Parker had already arrested Quinby two weeks before the assault – and despite being allowed to go free by Richard King – Parker had no lawful authority to re-arrest Quinby. Davis counter-argued, that according to witness statements, Parker never once

95.

announced that he was there - at the blacksmith shop that fateful day - to arrest Levi Quinby. But, Quinby's debt was Quinby's business and had little bearing upon Drew's case, only upon his claim that he was protecting a friend.

The defense then argued that Deputy Parker broke into the blacksmith shop by forcing open the door and that Joseph Drew had the right to protect his property, his place of business, from illegal entry. But Davis countered that the shop was not owned by Drew but by Daniel Conant and thus Drew did not have the right to defend a property that was not his own. Then, citing the testimony of witnesses in the court, Davis argued that Deputy Parker never entered the shop, but had remained out on the sidewalk and that Drew had stepped out of the shop and onto that sidewalk to confront Parker. Therefore, if Parker had never entered the shop then how could Parker have been a threat to the well-being of the property, causing Drew to defend it?

The argument of the defense had been weakened at each step in the trial, thus far. And Davis' case had remained strong. As the afternoon evolved into the evening, crowds continued to gather outside the Meeting House, as they awaited word of the verdict. Runners were still earning pennies retrieving information, though many of the hawkers of wares and other sales had called it a day, packed up, and gone home.

As the case continued, the defense was making its case for the lesser charge of manslaughter and worked diligently and methodically to weaken the charge of murder. The defense argued that passion in the heat of the moment had held more of a presence in the assault upon Parker than had intent, and that since the matter of intent to murder had to be present to conclude a charge of murder, Drew could not be convicted of the more serious crime. But, the prosecution – in essence – argued that one blow struck was passion, but three repeated blows were struck against Parker by Drew. And, that Drew had exclaimed his intent through his many comments made both before and after the fatal assault. Then, the defense also claimed that since Parker did not die immediately, but lingered for a week more, the charge against Drew should not be murder but the lesser charge of manslaughter. By late in the evening, both the prosecution and the defense had made their arguments, questioned the witnesses, cited case laws, and reviewed the evidence at hand. Then, as nine o'clock that evening neared, Daniel Davis, Nicholas Emery, and John Holmes each rested their cases.

Chief Justice Parsons then turned to the jury and charged them with their duties and the two counts of criminal charges they were to consider. In the matter of the first count, the willful murder of a deputy sheriff in the lawful execution of his office, the jury was directed that they could decide that Deputy Parker was not acting within the lawful execution of his office, as he had already arrested Quinby once on a warrant of the court. That as an agent in the service of the deputy Richard King had allowed Quinby to go free, and that since King was an agent in the service of Parker, Parker would have to honor King's action. Parsons directed the jury that should they believe this be the case, that Deputy Parker then had no lawful authority to again seize and re-arrest Quinby, and that the charge of murder could not be found.

On the second count of murder, the jury was to consider that Joseph Drew did murder Ebenezer Parker, a simple citizen of the Commonwealth of Massachusetts, not acting in any official capacity and that Joseph Drew – according to the evidence and testimony presented in court – was guilty of having killed Ebenezer Parker. Chief Justice Parsons then continued to explain, that should they find Joseph Drew guilty of killing Parker, they must then consider whether Malice Aforethought, a clear intention to commit the crime, was present. Should the jury determine that Malice aforethought was indeed present then the jury was to return a verdict of guilty of murder. Should the jury determine and find that no malice aforethought was present then the jury should return a verdict of guilty of manslaughter.

Yet, another matter also had to be decided by the jury. Parsons instructed these twelve men to consider and decide if the weapon used by Joseph Drew was, in fact, a deadly weapon in which the use of would cause death or great bodily harm. The weapon used could be a determinate in the conclusion of intent, as any weapon not likely to cause death or great bodily harm would suggest that intent to kill was not present. However, the use of a weapon likely to kill or do great bodily harm would indeed show intent to murder. And, there was something else to also be considered. The jury was to consider if Ebenezer Parker, as Drew's defense attorneys argued, was trespassing and whether he had illegally attempted to enter the blacksmith shop. Should the jury decide this matter was indeed the case, then – as the defense argued – Joseph Drew had a right to protect and defend his shop. Should the jury so decide that was indeed the case, then they were to decide if Joseph Drew had a right as an employee to protect and defend the blacksmith shop, when the shop was actually owned by Daniel Conant and not by Drew himself. Should either of these mitigating circumstances be found true and present by the jury, then a verdict of guilty of manslaughter, and not of murder, was to be delivered to the court.

At nearly ten o'clock that evening, Justice Parsons heard the foreman of the jury deliver its verdict. In the first count, the murder of a Deputy Sheriff in the lawful execution of his office, the jury found Joseph Drew not guilty. It appeared the jury did not have enough proof of why Parker was there or what had taken place between Parker, King, and Levi Quinby, two weeks before the assault in Saccarappa, by which to make a clear determination of whether or not Deputy Parker was acting within the lawful execution of his office or if he even sought out Levi Quinby, on January 11th, for the purpose of arresting him, demanding monies from him in order to settle the debt or to subpoena Quinby for another matter. The jury had far too little information to do anymore with the first count against Drew than to find a verdict of not guilty and move on to the second count.

In the matter of the second count, the Murder of Ebenezer Parker, the jury had decided that the weapon – a pitchfork handle – in the hands of a young and strong man such as Joseph Drew, was indeed a deadly weapon likely to kill or cause great bodily harm. And, the jury also considered the matter of Drew's intent and found that his comments – both before and after the assault – coupled with the fact that he delivered three forceful blows, proved his intent was indeed to kill Ebenezer Parker. And, the fact that immediately after Drew delivered the fatal blow, and Parker had fallen, the defendant showed no signs of remorse, had also solidified the jury's belief that his intent was indeed to murder Parker. The jury had decided that manslaughter was a lesser crime that did not warrant its finding and the foreman delivered the jury's unanimous verdict. Joseph Drew was guilty of Murder.

Chapter Nine

It is considered by the Court here, that the said Joseph Drew be taken to the Goal of the Commonwealth aforesaid from whence he came, and from thence, to the place of Execution & there to be hanged by the neck until he be dead.

The Trial of Levi Quinby and
the Sentencing of Joseph Drew

On Friday, May 27th of 1808, the very day after Joseph Drew was tried and found guilty of murdering Ebenezer Parker, Levi Quinby's trial began. There was still a lot of interest in the matter, and the second trial was also held in the Second Meeting House. However, this time, there were many fewer people outside, waiting for word of the outcome of the case. It seemed the people of Falmouth Neck had little concern about Levi Quinby. The rumors had spread for months that Quinby was a coward and a shirker, a man who avoided his responsibilities. The story of Drew's heroic action had been told and retold, over and over, for many months since the January assault. And, in almost every telling, Quinby was said to have cowered in a corner, inside the blacksmith shop, while his friend took up Quinby's defense. Now, with word spreading that

Drew had been convicted, many felt Quinby was the worthless cause of it all and not many seemed to care what happened to him.

When the trial began the defense team of Prentiss Mellen and Stephen Longfellow was ready for Daniel Davis. Mellen was an experienced and high-priced attorney and with the aid of Longfellow, a smart and able young legal mind, Davis would not have an easy time prosecuting Quinby. And, since the majority of the evidence that was about to be used against Quinby had already been introduced and given in testimony at the trial of Joseph Drew, both Mellen and Longfellow already knew what was coming. And, by the time the trial began, they already had Quinby's debt with Josiah Gould settled so that the genesis of the entire cause would not be a matter to rear its ugly head once again.

For Davis, his prosecution of the case relied heavily upon the testimony of the witnesses, who appeared again for a second day, to repeat the testimony they had given the previous day. Davis needed to prove that Quinby aided Drew in murdering Ebenezer Parker. When Drew had thrown the sledge at Richard King Drew remained empty handed and it was then that Quinby threw a club, which he had held in his own hands, down at the feet of Drew. And, Drew then picked up that club and struck the fatal blow to the head of Deputy Ebenezer Parker. And, proving intent wouldn't be difficult. It was testified to in court that Quinby had armed himself with a club, on the morning of January 11th of 1808, when he learned that Deputy Parker was searching for him. And, Quinby was heard saying that if Parker attempted to take him that he would break Parker's head.

The crux of the case against Quinby, much as it had for Drew, came down to intent. William Babb Jr., was sent into the blacksmith shop by Deputy Parker. He was a friend of both Drew and Quinby and he had wanted to calm the situation. And, when Drew stepped out of the shop to confront the deputies, Babb had remained within the blacksmith shop with Levi. He was now the sole witness to the actions of Levi Quinby and his testimony was key to either Quinby's prosecution or to his defense.

When Babb testified he was questioned again, and again, about Quinby's presence, his demeanor, and where he was in the shop when the assault, just outside the doorway, took place. Babb was asked over and over what Levi Quinby had said, or what he may have wanted from Drew. In the end, Babb testified that Quinby had said nothing the entire time of the incident. Babb testified that Quinby never left the forge and that yes, he threw down the club, but the club landed just inside the doorway. He also swore that because of where Quinby stood that he could not have seen a clear view of Joseph Drew or the deputies outside of the shop, and thus had no way of knowing that Drew's hand was empty after he threw the sledge. Mellen and Longfellow argued that Quinby could not have intended to fill Drew's hand with a deadly weapon when he could not have seen clearly that Drew's hand was empty. And, they proffered that had Quinby intended to rearm Drew that he would have stepped into the doorway and handed the weapon to his friend and defender, instead of tossing it to the ground some feet away.

When Chief Justice Parsons directed the Jury as to the charges they were to consider, the charges were much simpler than had been charged against Drew. The option of manslaughter was no longer to be considered as the charge of murder had been found by the jury in Drew's trial the day before. The first question before this jury was a simple one; did Levi Quinby aid and abet Joseph Drew in the murder of Ebenezer Parker? When the jury returned their verdict to the court the judgment was clear. The foreman of the jury announced that Levi Quinby was found Not Guilty! Sheriff Wait was then ordered to release Quinby and set him free.

> · **May 27.—Attended the trial of Levi Quin-by, who was indicted for murder and was acquited.**

Rev. Bradley's diary entry as it was transcribed by Leonard Bond Chapman, and appeared in Chapman's book *"Grandpa's Scrapbook."*

Then, on Saturday the 28th of May, Reverend Caleb Bradley escorted Mary Parker back to the Second Meeting House for the sentencing of Joseph Drew. On this day, the crowds that had descended upon Falmouth Neck just two days before had returned and the Meeting House was once again filled to the rafters with spectators. Again, Drew was marched through the streets from the Jail to receive the decision of the court. Many wondered if the justices would have mercy or whether they would remain true to the letter of law. Many in the crowd outside had wondered if Drew would be sentenced to life in prison at hard labor or be sentenced to something more drastic. And, each of those who waited in the Meeting House also wondered the same thing. Each of the attorneys were again present for this appearance in court, as were Sheriff Waite and the deputies of Cumberland County who escorted their prisoner to the Bar to hear Drew's fate.

When Chief Justice Parsons entered the temporary courtroom, followed by Justice Thatcher and Justice Sewell, no one could do anymore to help Joseph Drew, even Reverend Bradley could only pray for Drew's soul. But, the defense still had one more card to play. When the court was called to order, Holmes and Emery petitioned the court to delay the sentencing of their client. They offered that they had direct evidence that Richard King, Old Dick, had made prejudicial remarks before testifying as a key witness for the prosecution in Drew's trial. According to the attorneys, Old Dick had told someone that he, "would hang Drew with his testimony" if he could. And, the defense also had discovered that Jury member Ingalls had intended to vote "not guilty of murder" and instead wanted to vote "guilty of manslaughter." However, Ingalls felt some confusion as to his duty to vote with the majority opinion. Emery and Holmes felt their petition showed prejudice against a witness in giving testimony and irregularities in the jury's finding of guilt.

The petition submitted by the defense was a Hail Mary pass, a desperate last-ditch effort, to see their client's life spared, and it provided the court with an excuse to show mercy, should they wish to do so. But, Chief Justice Parsons only looked to his associate judges for a nod before telling the courtroom that the petition was denied. Parsons then explained that even if it should be proved that a prosecution witness meant for his testimony to damn the prisoner, the outcome of that proof would change nothing legally, for Joseph Drew. And, that despite Mr. Ingalls's confusion, even if he intended to change his vote in the verdict, it would now change nothing legally for the defendant. And, thus, since there were no legal gains to be made for the defendant, the motion or petition was denied. And, the Chief Justice then advised the defense that they had the option to appeal the sentencing and the verdict to the Governor of Massachusetts and ask for his mercy. With no other last-ditch attempts to be offered, Chief Justice Parsons ordered Joseph Drew to stand before the court to receive sentencing. As Drew struggled under the weight and encumbrance of the heavy chains of his bindings, he stood with the help of his attorneys. Chief Justice Parsons then began to read from his carefully prepared papers which lay on the table before him. The crowd, both inside the Meeting House and outside of the building, instantly quieted.

"Joseph Drew, the Jurors for the Commonwealth of Massachusetts, in the County of Cumberland, in the District of Maine, upon their oath, have found that you – Joseph Drew - not having the fear of God before your eyes, but being moved and seduced by the instigations of the Devil, on the eleventh day of January in the year of our Lord eighteen hundred and eight, with force and arms, did feloniously, willfully, and with malice

106.

aforethought, make an assault and deliver a mortal wound to one Ebenezer Parker, a Deputy Sheriff of the County of Cumberland – his being duly and legally authorized and empowered – to do and perform the duties of said office, and then and there being in the due and lawful execution of his office, in the peace of God and of the Commonwealth." Parsons then paused for a brief moment to turn the page on the table before him, and then he continued; "That said Parker did languish and live from the eleventh day of January to the eighteenth day of January, until he did die from the mortal wound received by you, the verdict against you was found by a jury to be that of guilty." Parsons then continued, "It is considered by the court, here, that you Joseph Drew be taken to the jail of the Commonwealth from whence you came, and from thence to a place of execution and to be hanged by the neck until you are dead."

May 28.—Attended court and heard the sentence of death pronounced by Judge Parsons.

Rev. Bradley's diary entry as it was transcribed by Leonard Bond Chapman, and appeared in Chapman's book *"Grandpa's Scrapbook."*

The sentence of death rang out through the Meeting House and was instantly delivered to the waiting crowds by young runners again earning their pennies. Gasps, cries, and a great deal of commotion immediately arose. Many had believed that Drew's life – the life of their Gideon - would be spared, even though the odds were against it. When Joseph Drew was walked out of the Meeting

House, surrounded once again by Cumberland County Deputies –
with swords drawn – a hushed silence fell over the crowd once
again. Drew looked upward and enjoyed the warmth of the summer
sun. meanwhile, the sound of Drew's chains rattling, with each step
he labored to take, filled the ears of onlookers. Slowly, either the
cries from Drew's supporters or jeers from the more prejudiced in
the crowd began to rise. Drew had his day in court and justice, many
had felt, had been served. For others, justice had been perverted and
showed no mercy for the man so many had considered their God-
sent Gideon, a hero of the downtrodden. Within a few minutes,
Joseph Drew disappeared from public view as he was escorted back
into the jail and placed back into the cell that had housed him for the
past five and a half months. Drew would not feel the sun shine down
on his face again for another two months.

For Old Dick King, the man who had witnessed Joseph Drew
deliver the brutal and mortal wounds upon the head of Deputy
Ebenezer Parker, his testimony did indeed help to see Drew
convicted and sentenced to hang. And, although there is no surviving
evidence to show how Ebenezer's widow, Mary Parker, had felt
about Drew's conviction and sentencing she must have felt some
sense of justice as she was escorted home from the Meeting House
that Saturday afternoon, after the sentencing of her husband's killer.
Though only assumptions can be made as to either the satisfaction or
the apprehension many felt at hearing Chief Justice Parsons deliver
the sentence of death by hanging, one man's sentiments were made
clear. In his diary entry, Reverend Caleb Bradley wrote, "Attended

trial of Drew… poor fellow… convicted of murder… heard the sentence of death pronounced by Judge Parsons."

For Joseph Drew, he had just one chance left to slip the hangman's noose, but the alternative was still not a rosy one. An attempt was being planned to apply for a commutation of Drew's sentence from death to life in prison at hard labor. The chances of success in this endeavor for mercy were slim, yet there was a chance. But, first, some changes had to be made. Drew would need a new defense team and he would need a great deal of support for his cause. Holmes and Emery were out as his legal defense team and Drew wanted someone who had demonstrated success and was willing to take on the new effort. The petition for commutation of the sentence would have to be made directly to the Governor of Massachusetts, James Sullivan, and there was little time to do so. Drew chose one man to take on this herculean effort and he chose one of the Falmouth Neck attorneys who was successful at freeing his friend Levi Quinby. Joseph Drew chose Stephen Longfellow to take up his cause and save his life.

Chapter Ten

The application cover for "The petition of Joseph Drew for pardon or commutation of the punishment of Death." Document image courtesy of the Massachusetts State Archives.

25 Men And Many Prayers

While Joseph Drew was returned to a jail cell, Mary Parker had a duty to settle her late husband's estate. When Ebenezer Parker was murdered he had still owned some acreage on the Gorham farm, an equal share left to him from his late father's estate. While the one-hundred-acre farm was divided among the surviving children and John Parker's widow, most of the farm had been bought back and left with Polly Parker Riggs and her husband William and their twelve children. Yet, Ebenezer still held ten and a quarter acres when he died and now Mary was – as Administratrix of his estate –

responsible for selling the land to help pay for any debts that Ebenezer had accrued at the time of his death. To help her handle these legal duties Mary Parker went into Falmouth Neck and hired attorney William T. Vaughan. And, her father-in-law – Ebenezer's stepfather – Benjamin Fickett took over as the eldest man in the Parker family. Fickett worked with Vaughan to gather an accounting of the debts and assist Mary in settling the bills.

While Mary was working to settle Ebenezer's estate, Levi Quinby was suffering troubles of his own at Saccarappa. Although the jury had found him not guilty of aiding and abetting the murder of Ebenezer Parker, and even though he was acquitted and freed, Levi Quinby still faced a much more discerning and less forgiving court; the court of public opinion. When Quinby returned to Saccarappa he had found a community that did not look upon him as a Gideon but as more of a Pontius Pilate, a man who willingly gave up his friend's life due to his own cowardice. And, since the assault five months earlier, much of the Quinby family's dirty linen had undoubtedly been aired out and allowed to run loose through the rumor mill. The story of Levi remaining in the blacksmith shop while Joseph Drew fought for his friend became a tale that told of Levi Quinby cowering in a corner. And, the unstable financial situation of cousins Henry and Frederick Quinby and their many debts had also become an anchor around Levi's neck. Levi Quinby was quickly finding it very difficult to live in Saccarappa.

For Joseph Drew, he was being visited daily by the local ministers of Falmouth Neck, all seeking to redeem Drew's soul and turn him toward God. Reverend Bradley was now visiting Drew daily and with God's Judgment Day fast approaching, Drew was beginning to see the wickedness of his ways and turn his heart towards the forgiveness of Jesus Christ. While Reverend Bradley was busy trying desperately to save the soul of Joseph Drew, Attorney Stephen Longfellow Jr., was trying desperately to save Drew's life.

On June 24th of 1808, Stephen Longfellow Jr., had amassed an impressive collection of twenty-five well-respected and noteworthy names, amassed upon a carefully worded petition for the "pardon or commutation of the punishment of death" of Joseph Drew. The noteworthiness of these signatories in this plea could not be denied. The very first signature was a man who had already had experience with hanging a murderer at Falmouth Neck, just eighteen years earlier, when he was the first United States Marshal for the District of Maine. Now, this Monmouth resident affixed his name to the very top of this petition, while he was in town to look over the new bridge that crossed over the Fore River, linking Falmouth Neck to Cape Elizabeth. But, this signatory was no longer the U.S. Marshal for the District of Maine: Henry A.L. Dearborn was now the sitting United States Secretary of War.

Another name that was noticed was the signature of Samuel Freeman, the Clerk of the Supreme Judicial Court, who presided in both the Drew and Quinby trials. Also of note, is the name

The original petition of Joseph Drew "for pardon or commutation of the punishment of Death," was submitted by his attorney, for Drew's appeal, Stephen Longfellow. The petition was submitted to Governor James Sullivan of the Commonwealth of Massachusetts, on June 24th of 1808. Courtesy of the Massachusetts State Archives.

George Bradbury, the sitting member of the Massachusetts House of Representatives for the District of Maine, and Samuel Bradley who was a selectman for the City at Falmouth Neck. Most of the signatories were either attorneys or merchants by profession and one man, Thomas Cross, had been a juror in the trial of Levi Quinby. Drew's current attorney, Stephen Longfellow Jr., signed the petition but neither of Drew's trial attorneys, John Holmes or Nicholas Emery, had signed the petition.

And, there was one other signature that is obvious today, which may have gone unnoticed at the time. The very last of the signatures, the twenty-fifth name signed at the very bottom of the petition for the pardon or commutation of Joseph Drew, was the signature of Mary Parker's attorney, William T. Vaughan. The five-page petition was also accompanied by a written statement from the confused Drew juror Isaiah Ingalls, who testified as to his voting in favor of a verdict of "guilty of murder" while under the influence of misconstrued instructions. The petition was then delivered to the Governor of the Commonwealth of Massachusetts, James Sullivan, for his consideration.

Cumberland County's High Sheriff John Waite couldn't hold off on his duties, to await the possibility that Governor Sullivan might commute the sentence of execution of Joseph Drew from death to life in prison at hard labor. The sentencing of the Supreme Judicial Court made his duty clear. Sheriff Waite had an execution by hanging to prepare for and the gruesome duty fell to him to see carried out. Sheriff Waite had to choose a location for the execution

114.

and he had to prepare a gallows for the hanging itself. He also had to insure that the discarding of Joseph Drew's earthly remains was also carried out. Cumberland County had allotted a total of thirty dollars for Sheriff Waite to operate and once the final order of execution, from Governor Sullivan, was in Waite's hands he had a limited time to see justice swiftly carried out.

Sheriff Waite knew, from the overwhelming interest shown by the community during Drew's trial, that a great number of spectators would show up to witness the execution. Waite had some experience with a public hanging at Falmouth Neck. In 1790, Sheriff Waite was in charge of jailing prisoner Thomas Bird, an English seaman, who was arrested and tried for Murder on the High Seas. It was a Federal case and one the United States Marshal for the District of Maine, Henry A.L. Dearborn, was duty-bound to execute at Falmouth Neck. Waite knew that many people would travel to Falmouth Neck to watch the hanging and he knew he would have to accommodate the large crowds. Waite chose a field next to the newly built Portland Observatory, on Munjoy's Hill, to hold the execution. It was just a short distance from the jail and an even shorter distance from what is now known as the Eastern Cemetery. Waite chose carpenters to build the gallows and men to dig the grave that would be the final resting place of Joseph Drew. With every detail being attended, Waite had only to await the arrival of the final order from Governor James Sullivan.

Fresh from his signing the commutation petition of Joseph Drew, attorney William T. Vaughan was handling the estate of

Drew's victim, Deputy Ebenezer Parker. Although Ebenezer's widow Mary Parker was the Administratrix of the estate Mary had difficulties in carrying out the task. Mary Larrabee Parker had not had any formal nor notable education and she was unable to read or write her own name. Now, Ebenezer's stepfather – Benjamin Fickett – the second husband of Hannah Roberts Parker, took over as Mary's agent and legal representative, to help settle his stepson's estate. The work of advertising for anyone who held notes of debt or claims against the estate had to be carried out, and claims had to be looked over, verified, and added up. The debts of Ebenezer Parker had to be deducted from the wealth of his estate and Benjamin stepped in to help Mary. Like most in the tough economic times of the Embargo, which continued to place all of America into a stranglehold of debt, Ebenezer had died "insolvent" with little wealth of any note, and some amount of debt. Mary remained on at Cape Elizabeth and was most probably living in the home of her in-laws, Benjamin and Hannah Fickett. Mary still had a toddler and a newborn son to raise and no income by which to do so.

While Levi Quinby was still finding his freedom to be a bitter-sweet existence in Saccarappa, Joseph Drew had little to look forward to. He was living his last days on earth and even the man

116.

who he defended had not come to visit him, nor had Drew laid eyes on Levi Quinby since the day Quinby had been taken from his jail cell to his trial on May 27th. It is believed that Drew's parents had visited their son, to say goodbye, and it is likely he was also visited by his former mentor, Blacksmith Abijah Feltch. And, the ministers of Falmouth Neck were also making daily visits to sit with Drew, to talk, and to pray. The Reverend Elijah Kellogg, Reverend Samuel Deane, Reverend Edward Payson, Reverend Benjamin Sawyer, and of course the Reverend Caleb Bradley, were all working feverishly to save the soul of Joseph Drew. Yet, as the month of June turned to July it was clear to all that the only man who could save the life of Joseph Drew was Massachusetts Governor James Sullivan.

Sullivan himself was also awaiting word. The Governor's Council on Pardons and Commutations was looking at the appeal of Joseph Drew and his request for mercy. The council had a duty to review the matter and was responsible for advising the Governor as to what actions, if any, the Governing Chief Executive of the Commonwealth of Massachusetts should take, or not take, in the matter at hand. And, the defense team for Joseph Drew had held a possible ace in their hands. Prentiss Mellen, the defense attorney who co-represented Levi Quinby in his trial, was a member of the Governor's Council. It seemed likely he would vote in favor of a commutation of sentence and would plead Drew's case within the council chambers. Also, one of the twenty-five signers of Drew's petition to the governor, Ezekiel Whitman, was a sitting member of the Massachusetts House of Representatives for Cumberland

County. Along with the signature and support of the sitting Clerk of The Superior Judicial Court during the Drew trial, and the support of one of the jurors, the Defense team felt they had a good chance of gaining a commutation of Drew's sentence from one of death by hanging to a sentence of life in prison at hard labor.

In the end, it appeared that none of the aces held up the sleeve of defense attorney Stephen Longfellow Jr., had made any difference. By July 15th, the council had met and fully addressed the petition for the pardon or commutation request of Joseph Drew. And, by the end of the day, a decision was made by the council. Governor James Sullivan was "unanimously advised that a pardon or commutation be not granted." In the end, it appeared that not even Prentiss Mellen had voted in favor of commutation. Governor Sullivan was a tough governor who had publicly condemned cases of retribution against law enforcement officers who were in the performance of their duties, according to the law, and he had also publicly stated that he would take a hard line against such unlawful retribution. With the unanimous recommendation of his council in hand, Governor James Sullivan deferred to their recommendation and immediately instructed William Tudor, the Secretary of the Commonwealth, to dispatch to Cumberland County Sheriff John Waite a formal warrant ordering the execution of Joseph Drew.

The Parker Farm at Gorham today. Originally Lot #30, is located at the corner of Longfellow Road and Brackett Road. Image courtesy of Google Earth.

Mount Pleasant Cemetery, in what was Cape Elizabeth Maine, now South Portland. This photo was taken sometime between the building of the second church in 1834 and the ground leveling work in 1875. The image shows the unlevel surface of the cemetery with heights and troughs present. Image courtesy of the South Portland Historical Society online.

Mount Pleasant Cemetery today, photo taken near the "long Parker lot."
The ground today is level, a result of the 1875 hard work of the MPC Trustees.
Image courtesy of the author.

On March 27th of 2023, Cumberland County Sheriff Kevin Joyce welcomed a few
of Deputy Ebenezer Parker's descendants and updated them on the effort to locate
their 5th and 6th great-grandfather. On the left, Sheriff Joyce explains the details of
the cold case. On the right, author Lori-Suzanne Dell explains the relationship
between the existing graves and those believed to be in the adjacent "long Parker
lot." Images taken by Courtney George and appear courtesy of the author.

Author and historian Lori-Suzanne Dell, standing over the proposed "long Parker lot," explains the details of the burials to Sheriff Joyce and the Parker Family. From left to right; Dell, Sheriff Joyce, Mike Herdan, Judy Herdan, and Mike Herdan. Image taken by Courtney George and appears courtesy of the author.

From left to right: Cumberland County Sheriff Kevin Joyce. Parker descendant John Herdan, Author/Historian Lori-Suzanne Dell, Judy Herdan, Parker descendant Mike Herdan, and Cumberland County Sheriff's Office Chief Deputy Naldo Gagnon. Image by Courtney George and appears courtesy of the author.

The former location of Conant's Blacksmith Shop today, now the former Guidi's Diner, at 916 Maine Street in Westbrook, Maine. Parker descendants, from left to right: John, Judy, and Mike Herdan. The diner steps are roughly where Drew exited the shop to assault Deputy Ebenezer Parker. Image courtesy of the author.

Chapter Eleven

The Execution Warrant cover that was sent to Cumberland County Sheriff John Waite. Courtesy of the Massachusetts State Archives.

The Execution of Joseph Drew

On the morning of Thursday, July 21st of 1808, the Eastern Argus newspaper had been published, and copies were being sold early in the day. A notice in the newspaper announced the time and location of the day's big event. The article ended with the statement that at three o'clock that afternoon Joseph Drew "…will be launched into eternity."

There is no indication if Mary Parker had left Cape Elizabeth on that hot summer's day to venture into Falmouth Neck to witness the execution of her husband's murderer. Yet, Reverend Caleb

123.

Bradley most assuredly was there. Not only had Bradley been working on Drew's soul, but Bradley also became a huge part of the day's spectacle, as would another local minister, Reverend Payson. The crowds were already gathering that morning and were slowly filtering into Falmouth Neck throughout the remainder of the early part of the day. Lemuel Moody's field, next to the newly built Portland Observatory, was filling-up at a rapid rate as onlookers, vendors, and hawkers of all sorts of wares and goods arrived. Much like the day of Drew's trial, nearly two months earlier, his execution was also becoming a local spectacle. Many spectators likely spread out picnic blankets and brought along baskets filled with fried chicken, cakes, cookies, potato salad, and other homemade goodies. Women would have been dressed in their finest summer dresses and men likely wore their best Sunday "go-to-meeting" clothes.

For those who had not yet found, or could not locate, a spot in Lemuel Moody's field with which to watch the execution, many spectators found other places to witness another sight, one also worthy of beholding. There had been a parade-like atmosphere that had gathered from the field - alongside the Observatory on Munjoy's Hill – up and down both sides of Congress Street, all the way to the courthouse, where the jail was housed outback. These crowds gathered and lined the roadway to witness Joseph Drew being marched to the gallows. It would be his final walk, in this life, and a final time when the sun would shine on his face. And, though it is unknown if Mary Parker was there to witness her husband's killer receiving his just punishment, there was one person who it is certain was not there; Levi Quinby.

It appears that by July of 1808, Levi Quinby had found life in Saccarappa to be untenable. Quinby had become a pariah in his own community, an unwanted man who became chastised by many, ignored by most, and seemingly despised by more than a few. Earning a living, despite the difficulties of the embargo, had become even more difficult and nearly impossible for Levi. Even Daniel Conant could not maintain Levi Quinby as an employee without suffering the consternation of others and the possible loss of customers. Levi had been labeled as a coward, a shirker, and as worthless. Levi had, by all accounts, not been to visit Joseph Drew since he had left Jail on the day of his own trial. And, with Drew about to give up his life for his friend, many still blamed Levi Quinby for the coming death of their Gideon. And, since Levi was exonerated from the murder and freed from jail, many believed that it was his family's wealthy connections that had helped him to escape what poor Joseph Drew could not afford to. Evidence shows that by July of 1808, Levi Quinby had abandoned Saccarappa and Cumberland County and relocated to Bangor, some 135 miles to the north where he had hopes that no one there had ever heard of Levi Quinby.

That ominous morning, Stephen Longfellow Jr., had gathered up his notes and documents and prepared to visit Joseph Drew for the last time. Stephen bid his eldest son - young Stephen - a good day, and then he kissed his wife Zilpah, whose arms were full with

125.

the couple's second son Henry Wadsworth – just over a year old.
Then, Longfellow walked out the front door of their Congress Street
home. He found a lot of pedestrians on the sidewalk that morning, all
seemingly headed to find a perfect perching place to witness the
day's events. Longfellow made his way to the courthouse, just a few
blocks away, where he entered and walked through to the jail. There,
Longfellow undoubtedly found Reverend Bradley sitting with
Joseph Drew. Longfellow had much to discuss with Drew, who had
been busy dictating his life story and his confession to the old
curmudgeon of a minister. Drew had indeed come to repent for his
wicked life, and the sinful ways in which he lived and would now
die. He was now, in the face of his own mortality, remorseful for the
murder of Deputy Ebenezer Parker. Yet, it was now too late for all
of this. Though it would appear that Reverend Bradley did finally
fulfill his Christian requirement to save the soul of his sorry
blacksmith, there was nothing that could now save the life of Joseph
Drew, and it was the sad duty of Stephen Longfellow to tell his
client this awful and harsh reality.

Also present in the jail was
John Waite, the High Sheriff of Cumberland County, whose duty it
was to see that the execution of Joseph Drew was properly and

legally carried out. The warrant signed by Governor James Sullivan sat folded up in Waite's pocket, and the full and macabre duty now rested in the hands of the seventy-six-year-old Sheriff. Between the Sheriff's Office and Governor Sullivan's Office, all of the details had been seen too, and there was little left to do but carry out the execution. It was now nearing noon and Joseph Drew was handed a white gown and cap, the costume for his death, which he put on. Then, manacles and chains were once again reattached to the body of Joseph Drew. Once dressed, not only were his ankles once again shackled to chains that connected to a chain belt around his waist, but his hands were also shackled to the chain belt. However, unlike the other times when Drew was shackled, this time Drew's collar manacle was left off. Instead, the hangman's noose was placed around Drew's neck and the coil of rope, which would stretch out over the frame of the gallows, was coiled and placed in Drew's chained hands. Drew would have to carry the heavy rope all the way up to the Observatory.

Outside the jailhouse a wagon and driver, with one lone horse, awaited. On the back of the wagon sat a plain, pine coffin. When Joseph Drew stepped out of the jailhouse, into the warm and sunny outdoors, he immediately looked up, and closed his eyes, to feel the sun's rays as they shone down upon his pale and drawn face. He was holding the thick coil of rope, and the white stocking cap was perched atop his head. He was barefoot and he wore the white gown he was given. A large contingent of deputies emerged from the jail and surrounded Drew and the coffin-bearing wagon. Then

Sheriff Waite and Reverend Bradley both emerged through the doorway. Sheriff Waite stood to the right side of Drew while Bradley stood to the left. Drew then looked ahead and saw the wagon before him and took note of the coffin that would he would soon lay in, for the rest of eternity. Drew then closed his eyes and lifted his head once again to feel the sunshine on his face. The Deputies then drew their swords and the wagon driver snapped the reigns telling the horse to move forward. Once again, the sound of Drew's chains could be heard as they jangled with each step that he took.

The procession moved slowly around the courthouse and out onto Congress Street. A hush fell throughout the group of static onlookers as the slow and somber procession approached. Many began saying prayers, some gently tossed flowers onto the street, and more than a few bowed their heads. Reverend Bradley had chosen many different passages from the bible, which he had specifically chosen for the occasion, and he read these passages aloud for the entire journey to the gallows. Most likely, each passage had more meaning for Bradley than it had for Drew. While Joseph Drew continued to look up to feel the sun's rays upon his face, the glint of the sun had flashed off the metal of the swords held by the deputies. The sounds of the horse's hooves radiated as they clopped along the roadway. The movement of the wagon as its wheels rolled over the ground added to the jangling of Drew's chains. Within minutes the procession passed by the old cemetery at the bottom of Munjoy's Hill, where Drew would soon be laid to rest. Drew likely noted the significance of the passing as the wagon and procession now began the climb up the hill to the Observatory. As the procession passed the hundreds of curbside spectators the masses stepped out into the road and followed behind the slow-moving cortege.

There were nearly four to five thousand, by some accounts, who had come to Falmouth Neck that day to see Joseph Drew "launched into eternity," and the majority of these people all gathered in Lemuel Moody's field next to the new Portland Observatory.

The Portland Observatory and Lemuel Moody's Field, about 1846.
Photo courtesy of Maine Historical Society.

When the procession made the turn off Congress Street, into the crowded field, a noisy - voice filled – outdoor arena fell silent.

Again, all that could be heard was the horse, the wagon, and the chains of the condemned. As the wagon neared the gallows ahead, the deputies began to clear spectators and obstructions from their path. When the procession reached the gallows, the wagon pulled around to the rear and came to a stop. The deputies then surrounded the gallows as Sheriff Waite led Joseph Drew, followed by Reverend Bradley, up the steep wooden steps. As Drew stepped up onto the stairs of the gallows his feet left the earth for the last time, as he ascended to the platform above.

Atop the gallows the Reverend Payson awaited. He had prepared himself for the day, with prayers and a sermon, to be delivered to the crowds. It was now one o'clock in the afternoon and Joseph Drew still had two hours by which to live. He was moved into position in the center of the platform, over the secured trap built into the deck, and the coil of rope was finally taken out of his arms. The cord was then thrown over the scaffold frame that stood above the gallows and the end of the rope was securely fastened. Joseph Drew then looked back up into the sky. Many thought Drew was deep in prayer, but Joseph Drew was once again enjoying the feeling of the warm summer sun upon his face. Then, the Reverend Payson launched himself into a two-hour course of prayers, with many biblical quotations, and numerous dire predictions all warning against sinful ways and wanton lifestyles. Payson spoke of evil and he spoke of gluttony, greed, corruption, and everything he could think of that was considered a mortal sin. Joseph Drew just stood absorbing the sunshine and was likely thinking of happier times.

When Drew's last two hours had eventually passed and three O'clock had finally arrived, Reverend Payson wrapped up his marathon sermon, and the official lawful proceedings of the execution then began. Sheriff Waite stepped forward and read the verdict of the Supreme Judicial Court and the finding of the jury. Waite announced that the jury had found Joseph Drew guilty of murder with malice aforethought, and read that Chief Justice Parsons had declared the punishment of death by hanging shall be administered. Waite then read from the warrant of execution signed by Massachusetts Commonwealth Governor James Sullivan. The requirements had been accomplished and the proprieties had all been observed. Waite then looked at his pocket watch and saw the time. There were two minutes left for Drew to live. Waite then looked down to the crowd nearest the foot of the gallows, to the face of Stephen Longfellow. Longfellow looked up to Waite and nodded. No last-minute reprieve had been delivered. The rope around Drew's neck was adjusted and Drew was re-centered on the trap door upon which he stood. Drew was asked if he had anything he wished to say, and Drew could only bring himself to state – as his face looked upwards to soak in the rays of the sun – "Oh! Life is sweet!" Then, the bells of the Second Meeting House could be heard ringing from just a half mile distant: It was three O'clock.

When the last bell rang, Sheriff Waite pulled back the lever, the trap below the feet of Joseph Drew swung open with a banging sound, and Saccarappa Blacksmith Joseph Drew plummeted through the scaffold deck. His body yanked downward to a fatal halt as his body shuttered and jerked. Gasps, cries, shrieks, and screams, came from the thousands who watched Drew as he dropped into the afterworld. Some women fainted, many began crying, some were inconsolable, and more than a few began praying. Nearly all were insensibly shocked and inconsolably horrified by what they had witnessed, though it is inconceivable exactly what it was they thought they would witness. It is said that Drew's body remained hanging for a few minutes while the last twitches and shutters emanated from his cooling corpse. Then, a doctor – believed to be Nathaniel Coffin Jr. - stepped forward and examined Joseph Drew and officially pronounced him dead. The deputies then placed their swords into their sheaths and helped to remove the lifeless body of Deputy Parker's murderer from the rope that had just exacted a final judicial revenge. Drew was then placed into the coffin on the back of the wagon, where the sun shone down upon his face one last time. Then, the coffin's lid was moved into place, eliminating the sunshine, and the coffin was permanently nailed shut.

The ministers and Sheriff Waite had removed themselves from the gallows and now made up the funeral procession of Joseph Drew, whose remains now had to be escorted to his grave. When the wagon moved around the gallows, and back into the large crowd of stunned onlookers, silence - except for the sobs and cries of saddened spectators – was joined with a semi-respectful reverence for the dead. Crowds moved back without coaxing and allowed the cortege to pass peacefully. Slowly, the procession moved down Munjoy's Hill to the old cemetery and entered the old burial ground.

Drew's open grave awaited on the very outer edge of the cemetery, where criminals, Quakers, and blacks, were usually buried. Joseph Drew's casket was placed in the grave and buried in the cool soil. No headstone was ever placed, or any sort of a marker, to denote his final resting place. Convicted criminals, especially murderers, were not generally granted such final reward or recognition as the honor of a headstone. Drew's grave would soon, in time, be lost for all of eternity. However, the legend and the myth of the life and death of Joseph Drew would survive and live on for over two centuries to come.

Chapter Twelve

The Eastern Argus announced the expected execution of Joseph Drew in the July 21st edition, which was published on the morning of Drew's hanging.

The Aftermath

If the newspapers had given little coverage to the assault or death of Ebenezer Parker, or the arrest of Levi Quinby or Joseph Drew, they certainly gave ample coverage to the trials and the execution. The Portland Gazette, for Monday, July 25th of 1808, committed nearly half of the edition's third page to Joseph Drew. The execution itself was covered in smaller detail and fewer column inches, presumably because so many already knew about the execution from having personally attended the event, or from hearing of the hanging from someone who was there. Yet, the larger portion of the story contained an article titled, "A Sketch of the Life and Confession of Joseph Drew." The article gave the details of Drew's life, as told by him the day before his hanging. Without this "sketch," we would almost certainly know nothing today of Joseph Drew.

Although much can be read into the confession and the detailed account Drew gave, what is surprising is the overall ending of the story and the overwhelming amount of biblical reference and theological regard which is written into the article. It is almost certain that the article

THE LIFE AND
CONFESSION OF
JOSEPH DREW.

I JOSEPH DREW, was born in Shapleigh, county of York, on the 9th of October, 1783, and I lived with my parents till I was 18 years of age, without any outbreakings of depravity, as I recollect, more than what is common with many youths who live without God in the world. In this term of time, I was taught to read and write, and educated in the Baptift perfuafion of religion, if in any ; but having no conftant inftructor, I feldom attended meeting, and early contracted the habit of mifpending the Lord's day.

At 18 years of age, I was put to the Blackfmith's trade, with Abijah Feltch, of Limer-

was written by the pious Reverend Caleb Bradley. The sketch and confession of Joseph Drew was immediately syndicated and reprinted verbatim in newspapers throughout the United States. And, there was a lengthy poem that was also written by a witness to the hanging. Thomas Shaw, a Standish writer and poet, had a penchant for writing about unusual local deaths, and Joseph Drew fit his needs for a new story. "A Morning Song," a broadside poster, was printed and passed out, pasted up everywhere to be read, and later published in book form in 1815. The lengthy and overly religious story would help to cement the future sustainability of Joseph Drew's enduring legacy for centuries to come.

Many of the participants in the life and death of Ebenezer Parker, and of the trial and execution of Levi Quinby and Joseph Drew, would go on to have noted futures. However, for at least a few of these legal participants, the Joseph Drew trial and execution would be the pinnacle event of their careers. Chief Justice Theophilus Parsons had already had a fabled and storied career by the time the Drew case appeared before him in 1808. Parsons had been a school teacher for three years at Falmouth while he studied law from 1770-1773. Parsons was admitted to the Bar in 1774 and then participated in state politics. He was a member of the Massachusetts Constitutional Convention in 1779, and he was a delegate to the State Convention to ratify the United States Constitution in 1788. By 1806, he was appointed as Chief Justice of the Massachusetts Commonwealth Superior Judicial Court. By October of 1813, just five years after he passed his sentence on Joseph Drew, Parsons died in Boston at the age of sixty-three. Chief Justice Parsons is interred at the Mount Auburn Cemetery at Cambridge in Massachusetts.

Sheriff John Waite also had a storied career before the Drew case came to trial. Waite had been a resident of Falmouth since childhood and by his teen years had begun a love affair with the sea. Waite went on to become a ship's Captain who had been involved in many notable affairs, one of which would – many years after his death – be immortalized in the poem "Evangeline" by a young poet named Henry Wadsworth Longfellow. Waite became a Colonel in the First Regiment for the Defenses of Falmouth during the revolution. And, by 1775, Colonel Waite was made the High Sheriff of a then fifteen years-old Cumberland County Sheriff's Office. Once the Drew trial and execution were over this High Sheriff was ready to retire. By 1809, a seventy-seven-year-old Sheriff John Waite left public service. Waite died on January 20th of 1820 at the age of eighty-eight; just two months shy of seeing Maine receive its statehood. Sheriff Waite is buried at the Eastern Cemetery in Portland.

Daniel Davis, the Solicitor General for the Commonwealth of Massachusetts, the man who tried the cases against both Drew and Quinby, also had an ambitious career. At the age of thirty-four Davis was appointed as the United States Attorney for the District of Maine by President George Washington. Then, in 1801, Davis took on the position of Solicitor General of the Commonwealth of Massachusetts. Davis had, just two years before the Drew and Quinby cases, been involved in a highly volatile case in Boston in which he co-prosecuted a man for manslaughter alongside then Massachusetts Attorney General James Sullivan. And, Theophilus Parsons also presided in that case, and in that case, Parsons instructed the jury to consider the charge of manslaughter rather than murder. Davis and Sullivan lost that case when the defendant was found "not guilty," and a large-scale public protest broke out in Boston, as a result. Davis' career as a public servant came to an end when Governor James Sullivan died in office, just five months after the Drew trial ended, and Davis spent the rest of his life in private practice. Daniel Davis lived until October 27th of 1835 when he died in Cambridge, Massachusetts, at the age of seventy-three. Davis is buried at Cobb's Hill Cemetery in Barnstable Massachusetts.

Nicholas Emery may have failed in his co-defense of Joseph Drew, but Emery's life was anything but a failure. He became active in Maine politics and was an advocate for Maine Statehood. By 1819, Emery was a Delegate to the Maine Constitutional Convention and he served as the first Portland representative to the Maine State House of Representatives, a position he held for three terms. By 1834, Nicholas Emery was appointed as an Associate Justice of the Maine Supreme Judicial Court, where he presided until 1841. Emery also served the State of Maine as a negotiator for peaceful terms in the "bloodless" Aroostook War of 1839. Emery died on August 24th of 1861 in Portland, just ten days shy of his eighty-fifth birthday. He is buried at the Western Cemetery in Portland.

John Holmes had begun his political career before the Drew matter had ever come before the Bar, and he continued to pursue his political interests even after Drew's execution. By 1813, Holmes was elected to the Massachusetts State Senate and he served as a United States Congressman in 1816. He was an ardent advocate for Maine Statehood and he served as a Delegate to the Maine Constitutional Convention with Nicholas Emery. When Maine received its statehood on March 15th of 1820, John Holmes was elected, and served seven years, as Maine's first United States Senator to Washington. He then served as Maine's U.S. Senator again from 1829 to 1833. He then returned to Maine and was elected to the Maine House of Representatives for two years before accepting a position as the United States Attorney for the District of Maine from 1841 until he died in Portland on July 7th of 1843, at the age of seventy. He is interred at the Eastern Cemetery in Portland.

Prentiss Mellen went on to a local and legendary status all his own. Although his fledgling legal practice assumingly picked up after his winning representation of Levi Quinby, Mellen had already begun his political career when the trial came to court in May of 1808. And, despite being a member of the Massachusetts Governor's Council in 1808, it appears Mellen began focusing more on his law career after Quinby's trial. By 1817, Mellen became a Trustee of Bowdoin College and was elected a United States Senator in 1818. He resigned as a United States Senator from Massachusetts when Maine achieved statehood in 1820 and he accepted an appointment as the first Chief Justice of the Maine Supreme Judicial Court, and he served in that position until age forced his retirement in 1834. Prentiss Mellen died in Portland, at the age of seventy-six, on December 31st of 1840. He is interred in the Western Cemetery at Portland.

Stephen Longfellow went on to serve in the Massachusetts House of Representatives in 1814 and served as a member of the Bowdoin College Board of Overseers from 1811 to 1817 and as a Trustee of Bowdoin College in 1817. Longfellow was then elected as Maine's United States Congressman from 1823 to 1825. He then was elected to the Maine House of Representatives in 1826. He is the father of Maine's own American Poet Henry Wadsworth Longfellow. Among many other interests, Stephen Longfellow remained active in many local causes and continued to practice law until his death at the age of seventy-three, on August 29th of 1849. Longfellow was interred in the Western Cemetery in Portland.

For Levi Quinby, the remainder of his life was lived under the long and cold shadow cast by his part in the events leading up to the assault on Deputy Ebenezer Parker on January 11th of 1808. Ultimately blamed for the cause, taken up by Joseph Drew, Quinby never escaped a wretched legend as a debtor and coward. Shortly after the trial and conviction of Joseph Drew, Levi Quinby moved north to Bangor Maine, to escape public scrutiny. He eventually married a woman named Hannah and had two sons; Frederick and Nathan. Although he tried his hand at being a Trader, his career never amounted to anything more than being a laborer and his nefarious reputation ultimately followed him to Bangor. Eventually, Quinby settled at Searsport. He is believed to have died in his late thirties or early forties, not long before his widow remarried to his best friend, William Webb Jr., of Saccarappa, on October 24th of 1823. Thus far, Levi Quinby's grave has not been located and any further story of his life seems to have been lost to history.

Chapter Thirteen

The Parkers of Cape Elizabeth and the Widow Mary Parker

By 1809, as the justices and attorneys – as well as Levi Quinby – all moved on with their lives, Deputy Parker's widow and two young sons were struggling to move on with their lives without Ebenezer. By July 6th, Mary Parker was before the justices of the Court of Common Pleas at Falmouth. Along with her attorney, William T. Vaughan, she petitioned the court to allow her to settle the estate of her late husband, Ebenezer Parker. Ebenezer had also suffered from the debilitating effects of the Embargo of 1806 and its supporting Enforcement Act of 1807, which caused him to fall behind in his own financial dealings. However, his employment as a deputy sheriff had allowed him to make payments and remain current with his arrears. Yet, his death not only stopped the clock on his life but on his finances as well. Mary was an uneducated woman, unable to read or write, and now without any means or promise of support, she had a large amount of debt that she was now obligated to see paid.

When Mary's petition to the court was submitted the papers enumerated Ebenezer's debts. The accounting proved that the debts had overtaken Ebenezer's wealth by nine hundred and twenty-eight dollars, and there seemed little accumulation of wealth to show for his life.

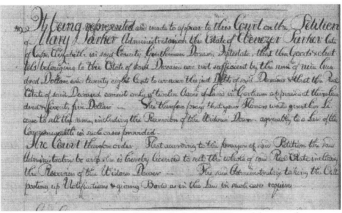

The Court's recorded entry of Mary's July 1809 petition to the court for permission to sell Ebenezer's assets to settle the debts of his estate. Record copied from the Court of Common Pleas, July 1809.

The court record only lists twelve acres of land in Gorham, his portion of his father's farm, which was estimated at a value of three-hundred and seventy-five dollars. There was no home or land listed as being owned in Cape Elizabeth, and it is assumed that Mary and the children were living with either her mother-in-law, Hannah Roberts Parker Fickett - and her second husband Benjamin - or with widower Captain Ebenezer Parker, who likely needed Mary's care in his elderly age. Soon after the case appeared in court, attorney

142.

Vaughan quickly placed the Gorham land up for auction to pay down the debts of the deceased. It was a hard sell. Not many, this far into the depression of Jefferson's Embargo, had the funds to buy land. Yet, one man did purchase Ebenezer's share of his late father's farm. By the first week of October of 1809, William T. McLellan of Gorham had purchased Ebenezer's section of the Parker farmland from Mary Parker. Although the court estimated the value of the land to be nearly four-hundred dollars, McLellan got the land for a rock-bottom price. McLellan paid just one hundred and twenty-five dollars. Even with the sale of the Gorham land, the estate was still just over eight-hundred dollars in debt. But, there was also a debt that was owed to the estate that needed to be settled. This debt, however, would be more painful for Mary to collect.

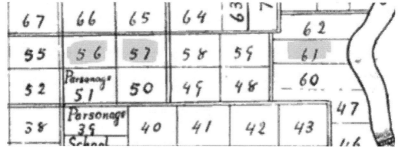

Lot #56 was owned by John and Elizabeth Warren Parker. Lot #57 was provided to William and Elizabeth Parker Larrabee by Ebenezer Parker. Lot # 61 became the farm of Thomas and Anna Parker Larrabee. Cropped edit of the Durham Property Map. Courtesy of the Durham Historical Society.

When Elizabeth Warren Parker's daughter Elizabeth set to marry Mary's nephew, William, Ebenezer Parker had arranged for the young couple to own a section of land between his late brother's Durham farm and his sister Anna's farm. Ebenezer had financed the purchase of the land for his niece and her new husband and Ebenezer had carried the debt. Now, the legalities of settling Ebenezer's estate forced Mary's hand. By December 5th of 1809, Mary Parker was once again before the Court of Common Pleas. She sued her nephew William Larrabee for a total debt of little more than five-hundred and forty dollars. According to the official court transcript, William Larrabee was a no-show in court, and the justices – by default - ruled for Mary. Assuming she was able to collect the amount owed Mary was still in debt for little more than two hundred and sixty dollars. There is no more evidence of a continued balance owed by Mary or the estate of Ebenezer Parker and it is assumed that the Parker family had somehow covered the remainder of the debt. Mary remained in Cape Elizabeth, raising her sons Nathaniel and Caleb, and it is assumed they remained with both Hannah and Benjamin, or more likely with Captain Ebenezer Parker, for some years to come.

When Thomas Jefferson left office, at the end of his second term as the third President of the United States of America, James Madison became the Chief Executive and Commander in Chief and he quickly endeavored to end the financial devastation of the Embargo of 1806 and 1807. A new Non-Intercourse Act of 1809 was passed and took effect. The new Act reestablished international trade with all nations, except for France and Great Britain. The financial depression of the Embargo of 1806-07 had finally come to an end for the still-youthful American nation. Trade relations between the United States and both of the excluded European Nations were not re-opened until the following year. However, while relations with

France slowly improved, negotiations and diplomatic relations with Great Britain continued to decay. And, the British Royal Navy still seized American ships and cargo and continued to impress American seamen into British service. Though there would be many more reasons, failures, and aims, which would be considered as direct – or indirect – causation, the new President and the new Congress had both had enough of Great Britain. On June 18th of 1812, Congress declared war on Great Britain, and the War of 1812, or the Second War for American Independence, had begun.

For the Parkers, like everyone else in America, many things had gotten better as the financial misfortunes of the economic depression finally eased. Yet, there was still pain and death to be had for the Parker family. On February 24th of 1813, Captain Ebenezer Parker's son Eleazer and his wife Elizabeth and their young son and three daughters were sleeping peacefully in their Standish home when an intruder silently entered the house. He came through a first-floor window, rummaged around the first floor, and then crept up the stairway to the second floor, where the family was all fast asleep. The intruder slinked through the hallway until he approached the bedroom where the young girls lay in the comfort and safety of their beds. Then, suddenly, the intruder attacked the eldest daughter. Hearing the commotion Eleazer awoke and ran to

145.

the bedroom and found a mountain lion standing upon his eldest daughter's bed. The cat had clamped the child's face into its jaws and Eleazer quickly grabbed the lion by the hind legs while the family dog also came to menace the cat. After a brief struggle, the cat also bit Eleazer, before it broke free of Parker's grip. As the girls ran from the room, the cat ran to a corner of the room to hide and was attacked by the family dog. Elizabeth quickly followed into the bedroom and handed Eleazer his gun. Eleazer quickly fired his musket and dispatched the cat, then saw to the care of his daughter, and his own wounds suffered from the fight with the rabid Mountain Lion. Within a week, Eleazer's daughter had died from the effects of hydrocephalus, and Eleazer also succumbed to the disease a few days afterward.

Back in Cape Elizabeth, word of the attack had reached Captain Ebenezer Parker and, despite his advanced age of approximately seventy-five, he wasted no time in rushing to Standish. He would remain for as long as it took to help his son's family recover from this insensible attack. Yet, when Eleazer and Eliza both died, Captain Parker had no doubt realized his time in Standish might have no expiration. There were two funerals to arrange, three children left to care for, a widow to help, and a farm to work on. And, Captain Parker's other sons Amos and Isaac also lent their hands and resources to help.

By February 1815, the War of 1812 was finally brought to an end with the signing of the Treaty of Ghent. Life in America was finally returning to a normal state which had not been known since

1806. The economy had already repaired itself, a usual and profitable byproduct of war, and many who served their nation were

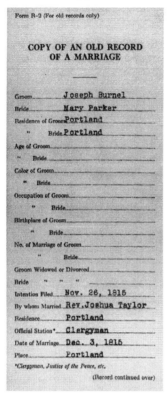

returning home. Mary Parker had been spending time with her sister-in-law, Deborah Parker Junkins, and her husband Isaac, at their home at State and York Street on Falmouth Neck. Little Nathaniel was now a boy of nine years and his little brother Caleb was just two years his junior. Ebenezer had been gone for seven years and Deborah and Isaac felt it was time that Mary ended her widowhood. Isaac worked as a shipwright, and he introduced one of his co-workers to Mary. When Joseph Burnell and Mary met, the coupling seemed to work. On November 26th of 1815, Mary Larrabee Parker and Joseph Burnell were married by the Reverend Joshua Taylor at a small ceremony believed held at the home of Deborah and Isaac Junkins. Mary's years of sole parenting and her worries over finances were now ended, and she was no longer alone. The new couple then moved to Bridgton, Maine, where Joseph and Mary settled on a small farm with Nathaniel and Caleb.

While Maine stood on the brink of statehood, the Parkers of Cape Elizabeth, once great in numbers, had now reduced to a small clan of leftovers. Just four years after Mary's marriage to Joseph, she once again found herself back at Cape Elizabeth, once again pregnant, and once again for the funeral of Ebenezer Parker, though this time it was Captain Ebenezer Parker who had died on January 15th of 1819, at the estimated age of eighty-one. By 1825, Mary Parker's father-in-law, Benjamin Fickett had also died at Cape Elizabeth. His wife, Hannah Roberts Parker Fickett, Deputy Parker's mother, then moved in with her daughter Deborah and her husband Isaac at Falmouth Neck, which was now the newly re-named, Portland. But, one year after Benjamin's death, Isaac Junkins also died and now both mother and daughter, both widowed, solely occupied the home. Yet Deborah and Isaac's son James was able to visit and help care for his mother and grandmother.

Although the Parkers of Cape Elizabeth had dwindled over the years since Mary's marriage to Joseph, Mary's brood at Bridgton was growing. With Joseph Burnell, Mary went on to have four more children; sons Alfred and Isaiah, and daughters Hannah and Joanna. However, on September 15th of 1828, Joseph Burnell suddenly died in Bridgton and was buried at the Forest Hill Cemetery. Mary was once again a widow, and now with four young children to care for. However, this time, Mary had two grown sons – 22-year-old Nathaniel and 20-year-old Caleb – to ease her burden. However, both Nathaniel and Caleb were still young and not yet earning enough to handle the responsibilities of a family, and though each helped their mother as best they could, Mary still found it difficult to manage her young family of four children. Hannah, the eldest child was barely eleven years of age, and the youngest was just seven years. Unable to keep the home she shared with Burnell, Mary was forced to "put her children out," to live and work for other families and to be better cared for. Although she would occasionally see her children, these Burnell children, as a family, would not again reunite.

On December 1st of 1830, Mary and Ebenezer's eldest son Nathaniel married Olive Emerson of Bridgton. One year later, on November 29th of 1831, Nathaniel's brother Caleb married Olive's sister Clarissa. But, in the first week of July in 1833, the last of the eldest generation of Parkers - ninety-seven-year-old Hannah Roberts Parker Fickett - had passed away at the Junkin's home in Portland.

With the marriages of both of Mary and Ebenezer's sons, a new generation of Parkers was set to be born at Bridgton. Nathaniel and Olive had given Mary Larrabee Parker Burnell her first of Ebenezer's grandchildren on January 9th of 1832 with the birth of Clarissa Delphina Parker. This was followed by a son, Charles Nathaniel, born on April 6th of 1834, and another daughter Laura, born on September 5th of 1838. And, Caleb and his wife Clarissa had also added to the list of new Parkers, with the birth of their daughter Mary on January 26th of 1835 and their son Ebenezer on December 29th of 1837.

By February 27th of 1842, Deborah Parker Junkins' son James had died of consumption in Portland. Deborah was now sixty-two years of age, a bit infirm, and alone with no one to care for her. Mary and Ebenezer's son Nathaniel must have felt a great debt or family responsibility was owed to this woman, the youngest sister of his father - Deputy Ebenezer Parker - as Nathaniel picked up his family and left Bridgton. They moved to Portland and stayed at the Junkins' home at State and York Street. Both Deborah's husband and her two children had died and she was completely alone. According to documents, Nathaniel sought to care for Deborah "for the rest of her life." And, shortly after his move to Portland, Nathaniel Charles Parker, started to forever reverse his birth name and go by the name Charles Nathaniel Parker. Deborah had then signed her house over to her nephew, and Charles and his wife and children took care of Deborah for the rest of her life.

Back in Bridgton, Mary was now sixty-five years of age and living with Caleb and his family. Mary now had a young brood of grandchildren to watch grow and that brood grew once more when Caleb and Clarissa welcomed their second son Nathan on May 6th of 1845. By Christmas of 1847, the Parker household in Bridgton was a full household. Caleb was now a man of nearly forty years of age, with a wife, three children, and an elderly mother to care for. He was a farmer and a trader who dealt much in real estate, much like his father had, and he is said to have operated a small grocery store on a hill in town, as well. The family had many things to be thankful for that holiday season and happiness in the Caleb Parker home was likely. Yet, on December 29th, just four days after Christmas, little Nathan took ill and quickly died of what is believed to have been pneumonia. He was just two and a half years old. On December 31st of 1847, the Parker family gathered to bury little Nathan in the Emerson family plot, at the High Street Cemetery in Bridgton.

Then, two years later, on February 26th of 1849, the woman who suffered so much, and had known so little security or happiness

in her life, also left the earth. Seventy-one-year-old Mary Larrabee Parker Burnell - also died at Bridgton. Caleb and his brother Nathaniel buried their mother in the Emerson Family plot near her grandson Nathan, at the High Street Cemetery. Then, on January 12th of 1851, seventy-two-year-old Deborah Parker Junkins died at her home in Portland, surrounded by her nephew Charles Nathaniel and his wife Olive and their three children. Deborah was buried next to her husband Isaac and their son James and their daughter Hannah, at the Eastern Cemetery at the foot of Munjoy's Hill in Portland.

By 1852, Caleb and Clarissa and Nathaniel and Olive had all sold off their possessions and lands and packed up their children. They had decided to leave Maine and start life fresh, at a westward location where new lands were inexpensive and future prosperity seemed assured. By late in the year, these descendants of Ebenezer Parker and Mary Larrabee had moved approximately one-thousand and three-hundred miles to the west and settled, to start a new chapter in the evolution of the Parker family, at Fond Du Lac Wisconsin.

Chapter Fourteen

Somerset County Sheriff's Deputy, Corporal Eugene Cole.
Image courtesy of the Associated Press.

Another Fallen Star

Just before 2 a.m., on April 25th of 2018, sixty-one-year-old Somerset County Deputy Sheriff Corporal Eugene Phillip Cole was on duty in Norridgewock, Maine, when he encountered a suspect that was known to law enforcement. John Williams was already free on bail for an unrelated weapons charge when Cole encountered the subject. Deputy Cole approached Williams to investigate the suspicious activity. Suddenly, Williams pulled out a gun and fired the weapon at the head of Deputy Cole, who died instantly. Williams then stole the Deputy's Police cruiser and fled the scene. Moments later Williams pulled into a convenience store, got a pack of cigarettes, and then drove away. For hours, law enforcement had searched for their missing deputy. At approximately seven-thirty that morning, Deputy Cole's lifeless body was discovered and a four-day manhunt for his killer began.

The media coverage of the massive law enforcement presence and action in Norridgewock was immediate and reports of the activity flooded television, radio, and internet airwaves. Camera crews, news anchors, and newsprint reporters all rushed to Somerset County. The local fire department had become the center of police operations as law enforcement agencies from the federal, state, county, and local levels all converged to assist. Game Wardens, state troopers, local Police, county sheriffs, and their deputies, agents of the Federal Bureau of Investigation, and many other state and federal agencies scoured the county. Law enforcement also appeared before cameras and put the word out that they were actively involved in a manhunt for an armed and dangerous John Williams.

The news coverage was relentless. Television programs were pre-empted in Maine as live reports and commentary went on and on, while Internet news coverage appeared to be non-stop. When the media seemingly had little else to say or nothing at all that was of new information, they inserted stories of the history of fallen officers in Maine. Nearly every reporter seemed to go out of their way to tell some portion of the story of Maine's first Fallen Star, Cumberland County Deputy Sheriff Ebenezer Parker, to balance out their live report of the most recent deputy who was now the latest of Maine's

Fallen Stars. Over and over, reporter after reporter, day after day, the name Deputy Ebenezer Parker was invoked, yet hardly anyone seemed to know anything about this deputy, the first in a long line of officers who would eventually sacrifice their lives in service to their communities.

On April 29th, a completely worn out and nearly naked John Williams had finally been taken into custody, a short distance from where he murdered Deputy Corporal Eugene Cole. When Williams was arrested his hands were bound behind his back with Deputy Cole's handcuffs. This new event only reinvigorated the media, yet now they were showing sympathy to John Williams whose appearance in a photograph - taken at the time of his arrest - made it appear that he had been beaten. Suddenly, the story was less about the deputy who gave his life to protect and serve and more about the poor and misfortunate, misunderstood, man who pulled the trigger. Yet again, the incomplete story of Deputy Ebenezer Parker was once again invoked over and over. The oft-repeated details of this deputy's life, and of his murder, were murky at best. Now, even that story veered away from the story of the fallen officer as the media turned to remember Parker's killer, Joseph Drew. However, those details, they seemed to get mostly right.

By the spring of 2019, as the trial of Deputy Cole's killer drew closer, more and more reports were being made about the legal arguments and legal-juxta-positioning between the differences between manslaughter and murder, before the trial. And, still, the vague details of Deputy Ebenezer Parker paled in comparison to the storied legend of his killer Joseph Drew. It was clear, that none of these reporters knew anything about Deputy Parker, but they seemed to know a lot about Joseph Drew. And, now with the trial of John Williams approaching, even the memory of Deputy Cole seemed to slip into a shadowy haze in favor of a new and bright spotlight that favored the accused. As a historian, I had already been somewhat familiar with the sacrifice of Deputy Ebenezer Parker and the mythical legend of Blacksmith Joseph Drew. I was also well aware of how a media frenzy in such a case had a historical habit of creating a scale-tipping disparity between fact and myth. I worried that in the case of Deputy Eugene Cole and the Killer John Williams, it was about to happen all over again.

From the first moment that Deputy Cole's murder had been announced I was heartbroken. I felt a deep sense of loss, both as an American and as a Mainer. I felt saddened for the fallen deputy, his fellow officers, and his family and friends. I felt the anguish his fellow law enforcement family must have felt at the senseless loss of this hero. And I felt anger, not only for the helplessness I felt at not being able to do something about it all but also at the prime media – celebrity-like - attention that John Williams was receiving for his heinous crime. I wanted to do something, but there seemed nothing I could do. Then, I saw yet another media report and this one featured a news reporter who stood at the Fallen Law Enforcement Officers Memorial in Augusta. This reporter stood before the cold, gray, granite wall of names of so many of Maine's officers, men who gave their lives in service to their state, their communities, and their country, all in the line of duty. And, there over the shoulder of the reporter was the name Ebenezer Parker. And, again, the reporter invoked the memory of Deputy Ebenezer Parker, yet he had little to say about the man himself. That's when I knew what I could do.

For the next few days, I mulled over the idea of what I would do, what action I could take, and how I could finally alleviate my feeling of helplessness and do something that could somehow make a difference. By mid-May, I was taking a bus ride in my hometown of Brunswick and talking to the driver, a man who had become a friend, and I was telling him about my thoughts. Verne Smith was a willing conversant and his feedback was always helpful to my thoughts. I told him that I knew there had been a long mystery that law enforcement had tried to solve, but had not been able to. They had long been searching for the final resting place of Deputy Ebenezer Parker, the first fallen officer to give his life in the line of duty in Maine history. It was an effort sparked by the establishment of the National Fallen Law Enforcement Officer's Memorial Foundation, and each law enforcement agency in America was tasked to find the graves of each of their Fallen Stars. When my talk with Verne was over, I had made my decision. I told Verne, I would contact the Sheriff of Cumberland County, I would offer my services as a historian, and I would set out to find the final resting place of Cumberland County Deputy Sheriff Ebenezer Parker.

By the end of the day, I had sent an email to Cumberland County Sheriff Kevin Joyce. Although I had met the man, informally, a few times over the years I did not know him nor did I have any reason to think he would remember me. So, I introduced myself and told him I was a historian and an author of books on Maine history, and that I wanted to offer my services in an effort to find Deputy Parker. A day or so later, I received an email from the Sheriff. He was on vacation but would be happy to get back to me once he returned to his office later in the week. However, he would be happy to have my assistance and he mentioned that his office had a binder full of materials he would be glad to share with me. I didn't mention that I had already begun to research the matter. I was already hip-deep in notes, dates, names, and modern-day retellings of the event from over two centuries prior to my start. I had already been to the library and signed out a bagful of books and had already begun a genealogical research. I had already bookmarked a dozen or more internet resources, web pages, and vintage newspaper articles, and had accumulated a vast list of other archives that I intended to look at.

When Sheriff Joyce returned from his vacation, we reconnected by email and set a date for me to visit him at his office so I could look at the binder of documents and other information that had been accumulated over many years. I was champing at the bit to look at this treasure trove of information. I was desperate for some clarity, some evidence of fact, to gain a toehold in reality. I had taken on this research project with the hunger of a wild animal in a desolate and food-starved land. I had spent sixteen to eighteen hours a day reading, making notes, and thinking about every morsel of information I was ingesting. I couldn't get enough. Being a historian,

I am used to the quandaries of research, and some of the confusion that can be found. I am also used to information voids and how to manage to fill those voids with primary source facts. In three decades of being a historian, I had become rather adept at making sense out of confusion and finding what seemed not to exist. However, everything I was reading seemed to be completely confused, often contradicting, with no basis in fact.

Trying to obtain just the basic information about the matter was immediately impossible. From modern-day telling to reports of old, everything was a quagmire of contradiction. Some reports had Deputy Parker dying in Saccarappa, today's town of Westbrook. Other tellings of the story reported that Deputy Parker died in Cape Elizabeth. Some reports said he was clubbed to death, one report stated that he was shot. One report said Deputy Parker was a man in his forties and another said he was in his twenties. One report said that he was killed by a man named either Quinby or Quimby, though most said Joseph Drew. Even the dates of Parkers death were inconsistent. Many reports gave January 11th as the date he was killed, some the 18th, yet the memorial outside of the present-day Cumberland County Sheriff's Office states January 15th. Some reports even gave the year of his death as 1806, though most stated 1808. Most reports varied and had Parker being either from Gorham, Durham, Scarborough, Portland, Falmouth, Westbrook, or Cape Elizabeth. There was little to no consistency in anything I was reading and none of the basic facts were dependable. What I had found in this cursory search was nothing short of a historian's nightmare.

Worst of all was the fact that I had not been able to even determine exactly which Ebenezer Parker I was trying to find. It appeared that the name Ebenezer was common in 1808, and I had located at least three Ebenezer Parkers within the area of Falmouth, for the same period. Then came a realization that there were two Ebenezer Parkers who were living in Cape Elizabeth in 1808. This deputy was a string entangled in a bird's nest of other strings, all tied, twisted, jumbled, and wrapped up – one with the other – in a massive ball that had no beginning and no end. How do I find an individual when I cannot determine just which individual it is I am looking for? I needed more detail, yet the details were sketchy and unreliable at best. When I finally examined the binder at the Sheriff's Office I discovered it to be full of copies of the same inconsistent records, retellings of rumors, and stories of the myth that I had already located in other searches. The toe-hold of reality I was struggling to grasp hold of was not there to be found, within the Sheriff's binder. It was now clear to me just why no one had much to say about Deputy Parker; he was lost in a shadowy swamp of historical quicksand. I now knew this would not be an easy matter of simple research. Finding Deputy Ebenezer Parker would be a historian's research challenge of a lifetime.

Chapter Fifteen

The memorial marker at the Fallen Officers Memorial in Augusta, Maine.
Image courtesy of the Author.

A Historian's Inquiry Begins

By the fall of 2019, I had already been to the Maine Historical Society in Portland and searched through the 1808 files of the Sheriff of Cumberland County, John Waite. And, I had perused through several other files that were maintained within their holdings. I had spent days online searching through current transcription lists of area cemeteries, and I had committed my nights to read through four years worth of newspapers from 1805 and 1809. And, I had read several histories that were published by other historians, which I borrowed from the Curtis Memorial Library. The good news was that after all of this effort, which had been expended over those past six months, I had finally narrowed down just which

Ebenezer Parker I was searching for. The bad news was I still had no idea where Deputy Ebenezer Parker was buried. I decided to launch a three-pronged attack. First, I would begin an in-depth genealogy of Ebenezer Parker and his immediate family, and then check the burial location of each family member to see if Ebenezer was buried in family plots, or nearby. Second, I would scour every pertinent cemetery in Cumberland County, which existed at the time of Ebenezer Parker's death, to look for any signs that Ebenezer might be interred there. And third, since it was painfully clear that this search would be a massive undertaking, I would seek to enlist as much assistance in this endeavor as I could obtain.

I also realized that I would have to become as much of an expert in the area of Cape Elizabeth, Portland, and Westbrook, as I could for the year 1808. I would need to know just how things worked, where things were located, and who was in charge, and I would need to know what the common experience was for those living and working in the area. I would have to be able to mentally transport myself to, and think in terms of, the time of 1808 as if I had personally lived there at the time. I began gathering as many books on the history of the towns and of the people living there, as I could find. I was now working on the Parker Inquiry seven days per week and all around the clock. Soon, I wasn't able to think or talk about anything else. I would read and research until I was too tired to continue. Then, I would take a four-hour nap, wake up, and make another pot of coffee, then go right back to reading and researching.

Then, another nap, and so on. The search for Ebenezer Parker had become an all-consuming obsession.

I immediately received the help of Jim Rowe, then the President of the Cape Elizabeth Historical Preservation Society, and I began emailing eminent cemetery historian and author Ron Romano. Jim was able to spread the word of my search efforts and soon Cape Elizabeth sleuth and historian Sally Jordan had joined in the search for details. And, I began calling upon the Maine State Archives at Augusta, and the Osher Map Library at the University of Southern Maine in Portland. And, since Maine was still a part of the Commonwealth of Massachusetts in 1808, I opened communications with the Massachusetts State Archive. I reached out to any location I felt could have some pertinent collection, document, file, or information on anything, anyone, or any details even remotely connected to Ebenezer Parker, Joseph Drew, or Levi Quinby.

I also contacted the Westbrook Historical Society. Surely this group would have details, facts, documents, or some information on one of the most heinous events in Maine history, which just so happened to take place in their town. However, the response I received to my query was less than helpful. It was downright dejecting. I was told that the Society had already searched their archives numerous times, after being asked by numerous others who tried to solve this mystery, and that nothing had ever been found. When I asked them to search again, with certain criteria, which I could provide, the reply I received was curt and dismissive. The answer was a brusque "no", with the reiteration that they had already done this search many times and that they would not do it again. The woman never returned any of the phone messages I left after this rejection, nor did she ever reply to any further emails or phone calls. The door at the Westbrook Historical Society was slammed shut.

I quickly encountered several people who were suffering from Parker fatigue. Numerous researchers or historians, who were the self-professed guardians of the historical archive gateway, had already labored far too often through endless inquiries, from numerous people who tried – over the years – to solve the mystery of Ebenezer Parker. They had no reason now to believe that this "Historian's Inquiry" would be any different or conclude with any better effect. Even though I had assured them I had already done so, they simply repeated the search criteria by typing into their computer browser search box, reading me the results, and then invited me to visit during regular business hours. I was perplexed. When did historians stop operating by the protocols and values we were taught in college? When did the computer search replace the hands-on, boots-on-the-ground, primary document search within the old, musty, archive basement? When had getting up and taking a look through the actual files become something we historians stopped doing? Though much of this case was still murky, one thing was painfully clear; if I was going to find anything important to help solve this case it wouldn't be found through a computer browser search box. It was going to be something completely overlooked and just waiting to be discovered.

I was able to locate two things online, however, in the holdings of the Westbrook Historical Society, that absolutely related to the mystery. I discovered two photographs of an old building, taken at the turn of the twentieth century, that was identified as having been a blacksmith shop dating back to before the revolutionary war. One photograph was an incredibly clear photograph of the side of a long, dilapidated, old wooden structure.

The former Conant Blacksmith Shop where the fatal assault of Ebenezer Parker took place. Image appears courtesy of the Westbrook Historical Society.

The Main Street view of the front of the blacksmith shop (center). Image appears courtesy of the Westbrook Historical Society.

The other photograph showed the front side of the building as it was sandwiched between a clothing shop and a carriage shop. And, the photograph identified the current-day location as a place that I was

164.

quite familiar with. I began performing a deed search of the property and had insured that it had indeed been a blacksmith shop. Now, I needed to begin yet another area of study of the era and people of another town, Saccarappa. As it would turn out, the woman who slammed the door in my face at the Westbrook Historical Society was wrong about not having anything relating to Joseph Drew, the assault, or the murder of Ebenezer Parker. They had two photographs of the scene of the crime. And, it would not be the only thing she was wrong about.

By 2020, a new challenge had deterred my efforts to solve the mystery that was resisting me at every turn. When the Covid epidemic spread like wildfire throughout the world, and here in Maine, it closed businesses, offices, agencies, and stores. It also closed libraries, archives, historical societies, governmental offices, and every other place that I needed to be open if I was to continue my search. Suddenly, I could no longer get books I needed to read, scour files or archival materials, thumb through maps, or access anything necessary to expand my knowledge. And, I was at a desperate point in the research. I was re-reading the newspapers of the time, once again, trying to find anything I could to help locate a clue or fact that would reignite my stalled progress. I had been accessing the old Eastern Argus and Portland Gazette newspapers at Bowdoin College, but the campus was now closed due to the pandemic. I contacted the head librarian and asked for special consideration. I told her I was assisting the Sheriff of Cumberland County and I copied Sheriff Joyce in the email, as I always did whenever I invoked his name in one of my emails. I asked her for a guest password and a link to the newspaper gateway. It's something that was commonly given to students and friends of the college and I felt, that as a historian - under such circumstances - the College would likely be eager to lend their assistance. Her answer to my request was a clear "no." By the end of the week the President of Bowdoin College, Clayton Rose, had received a letter from Sheriff Joyce. A few days later the head librarian contacted me with a username and password. Thanks to Bowdoin College, the research effort, temporarily thwarted by Covid, was once again underway.

Aside from the endless reading of old newspapers from the era, which now expanded to one-hundred and nineteen papers that spanned from Mississippi to Maine in the years 1800 to 1815, I was also continuing a physical search of area cemeteries. On July 7th of

2019, my friend and personal attorney, Vanessa Bartlett, and I started with a hands-on search of the Old Stroudwater Burial Ground Cemetery on the outskirts of Portland, and we included the Old Saccarappa Cemetery in Westbrook. Aside from sunburn, little else of note had been found. However, by the end of the search, the

Stroudwater Cemetery was eliminated as a likely burial place for Deputy Parker. And, although it could not be completely ruled out at the time, it was not likely that Saccarappa Cemetery was where

Ebenezer found his eternal rest either. However, while at Saccarappa cemetery we did discover the grave of William and Mary Riggs. Mary was also known as Polly to her Parker brothers and sisters, one of her brothers was Ebenezer Parker. In time, both William and Mary came to remain on what was left of the Parker farm at Gorham. The find brought me no closer to the finding of Deputy Parker's grave, but it did, once again, demonstrate that Deputy Parker's siblings all had standing gravestones.

Now, as 2020 continued, despite the restriction of the pandemic, I was able to continue the cemetery searches and had now eliminated the Gorham cemeteries as well. Many of Ebenezer's relatives were located but Ebenezer was still nowhere to be found. I had been to Standish and looked at the Parker burials, and to Durham to see other Parkers, as well as the Larrabees. Still, there was no sign of Ebenezer. But, one thing was beginning to become apparent; all of the Parkers and Larrabees were buried with headstones, and nearly all of the stones were still standing.

I had a fairly thorough genealogy of Ebenezer's immediate Parker family and they were easy to find. But, it was now clear that another two Parker family members were also missing. The graves of Ebenezer's brother John and their father Nathaniel were nowhere to be found. I had also scoured the Cape Elizabeth cemeteries, which existed in 1808, and found nothing. I then went to Scarborough, Portland, Falmouth, and Freeport. Still, nothing could be found that was helpful. I continued reading, continued searching for anything I could locate and I continued to contact every one and any place that

I figured might be able to help. I was perplexed as to why there was so little in the way of a news story about the assault at Saccarappa, which led to Deputy Parker's death. And, I couldn't find a thing about where Ebenezer's widow, Mary Larrabee Parker, might have been buried.

I was able to find several Mary Larrabees from the time and I began a process of elimination. Then, I stumbled across mention of a Mary Larrabee Burnell being a widow of a deputy who was killed, and the story mentioned that she later resettled in Bridgton. A search led me to information that this Mary Burnell was buried at the High Street Cemetery in Bridgton. I contacted the Bridgton Town Clerk's Office and explained who I was and what I was trying to locate. The Town Clerk then sent someone in her office to the cemetery with a cell phone. Later that day, I received images of a headstone that read "Mary Burnell. Relict of Ebenr. Parker" This led me to contact the Bridgton Historical Society, which led me to a few articles in the Bridgton News from the early twentieth century. The information in these  articles was greatly revealing, substantive, and direction-changing.

By 2021, the effects of Covid were still with us and were still thwarting the swift completion of my effort. However, despite the restrictions, I was making marvelous headway. I had a fairly complete genealogical map of the Parker family and I had a great deal of information about the assault on Deputy Parker. I knew more about the man himself, his family, his history, and his children. I knew who many of his descendants were, right up to the present day, and many of these modern-day descendants had been located and joined me on my Facebook page. They were all greatly interested in the details of the legend of their great-grandfather, which they had heard about, and they all wanted to know about the search I was conducting, and I was offering them daily updates. I had also been able to eliminate more cemeteries from consideration, and I had begun focusing on one likely cemetery as being a probable location for the burial of Deputy Ebenezer Parker. One of the articles that had been located in an old Bridgton News publication gave a very descriptive retelling of the story of Deputy Parker. Despite some inaccuracies, the accounting seemed to be quite detailed and many of the particulars aligned with details I had already learned elsewhere.

Months before finding this great article in the old Bridgton News, I had contacted the Tate Museum in Stroudwater. I had tried to determine if Dr. Jeremiah Barker of Stroudwater might have been the physician who attended to the injuries of Deputy Ebenezer Parker. In fact, I had spent quite some time researching the physicians at the time to see who might have looked after Parker, and who might have left their records to posterity for me to discover today. I had read about a talk that was held at the museum by Dr. Richard Kahn, who had just published a book about Jeremiah Barker, and I wanted to contact Dr. Kahn. I mentioned to the Museum what it was I specifically wanted to know and they passed along the message to the good Doctor. In about a week I had my response. He said that he had found no information in Barker's notes suggesting he had any dealings with Parker. However, Kahn suggested that with such an injury to Parker's skull that Barker – if he had seen Parker at all – would have sent Parker on to Portland to see Dr. Nathaniel Coffin Jr. Barker thought a great deal of Coffin and he knew that Coffin was the pre-eminent surgeon in the area when it came to the surgical "trephine" procedure that Parker would have undoubtedly needed. When I read the Bridgton News article on the assault on Deputy Parker the article told of "surgeons from Portland" being needed to "trephine" Parker's head wound. I knew then that I had finally found a news article that, despite a few small inaccuracies, had told the harrowing story of the death of Deputy Ebenezer Parker. And, the story appeared to be quite accurate overall. The article also told me something else, the location of where Cumberland County Deputy Sheriff Ebenezer Parker may have actually died.

I now had more information to look up. I now had to learn all I could about Dr. Nathaniel Coffin Jr., and I had to learn about the surgical procedure of trephining in 1808. Yet, the pandemic precautions were still in place, though starting to ease and lift. Limitations on research time allotted and days and hours of operation at libraries and historical societies made it nearly impossible to spend any quality time on research. And, if there was anything I could swear to at all, from what I had learned in this Inquiry, it was that everything – even the tiniest details – took quite a bit of time to research. Fortunately, there were enough downloadable online resources of published histories to help my effort. By the spring of 2021, I had determined that Dr. Coffin's office was located at, what was then known as, King and Middle Street in Portland. His office was in a rather large building that also housed his home. And, I learned that he often visited his patients at their homes. His office was quite close to the Parker Ferry and the Sheriff's Office, and just up the road from the home of Ebenezer's sister Deborah. And, the article described Parker's last moments and his death. It seemed appropriate that Parker likely had died at Dr. Coffin's Office.

I knew that Parker had died on January 18th of 1808. I also knew from a reprint of the Reverend Caleb Bradley's diaries in historian Leonard Bond Chapman's *Deering News* – that Bradley attended to Parker's funeral on January 20th, just two days later. Everything seemed centered in Portland. Parker's sister lived right down the road from Coffin's office and right in between was not only the Sheriff's Office but the Court House as well. And, right there in the Eastern Cemetery was where Parker's killer, Joseph Drew, was buried in July of that year. Dr. Coffin would eventually also be entombed there. Sheriff Waite was buried there, and one or two of the attorneys in the trial were buried there. And, there were other connections. Plus, Deborah Parker Junkins, Ebenezer's sister – and her family – were also buried there. And, right next to Deborah and her husband and two children was what appeared to be an empty space. Could this be the final resting place of Ebenezer Parker?

I was running on fumes by April of 2021. I was exhausted, physically, mentally, and emotionally. My diabetes was now out of control, I had gained thirty pounds, and I was smoking nearly two packs a day. My home looked like a paper-tossing elf had gone on a fit-induced spree, and I badly needed a vacation. Sheriff Joyce and I had often considered going public with the search for Ebenezer many times in hopes that word of the effort might dislodge some previously forgotten memory of something someone hadn't recalled in years. Maybe, going public might also bring about more assistance by drumming-up curiosity in the public. Many of those who had originally jumped in to help were now gone, had moved on to other projects, or just no longer had the time to devote to such a time-demanding effort.

Our search of the Eastern Cemetery seemed likely, yet yielded no final answers in the quest of the Historian's Inquiry. Photo: Courtesy WGME-13 News Video.

I was, for the most part, on my own by this point - though there was help, if I asked for it, from specific persons, for specific reasons. I had now eliminated all but two cemeteries from the 'most likely' search areas. One of these two cemeteries allowed me absolutely no indication that I should continue to pursue searching there. No documents or stories, and no rumors or anything else had pointed to South Portland, which in 1808 was still Cape Elizabeth. In fact, I had eliminated all the cemeteries in present-day Cape Elizabeth, and except for one cemetery, I had also eliminated all of the cemeteries in South Portland. With all of the information I now had at hand, and with all of the theory I could derive, I was sure that Eastern Cemetery was the probable location of Deputy Ebenezer Parker's final resting place. It just seemed to make sense. And, all of the roads of information appeared to end in Portland.

I immediately contacted Ron Romano, who is an expert on the Eastern Cemetery in Portland, having literally written the book on the ancient cemetery and having a leading role in the continued preservation of the burying ground. And, Sheriff Joyce had scheduled an interview with Brad Rogers of WGME-13, to go

public, in hopes of finding more information, more help, and to spread the word about our efforts. By mid-May, the National Law Enforcement Officer's Memorial weekend was approaching and the interview was held at the Sheriff's Office. Afterward, Ron and I went to the Eastern Cemetery with Brad Rogers for filming. A few days later, Ron and other preservationists of the Eastern Cemetery explored the vacant space next to the graves of Deborah Parker Junkins and her family. These dedicated volunteers excavated the Junkins' headstone bases and righted them, and did other preservation work on these terribly weathered stones. They also explored the space where it was hoped that Deputy Ebenezer Parker may have been laid to rest. When the work was complete, one thing was fairly sure; Deputy Ebenezer Parker was not there. Ron had spent time looking over everything he had in the way of facts, lists, and other supporting evidence. We spent a good deal of time emailing and discussing the likelihood of Parker being buried elsewhere in the cemetery at Eastern. In the end, Ron had little reason to now believe Deputy Parker was there, and in the face of his expertise and a lack of further evidence, I had to concur. Ron was an expert in this cemetery, and I had to concede there was little left to pursue there. Eastern Cemetery was now eliminated as well as many others. The question still remained; Where was Ebenezer Parker buried?

My exhaustion was now complete. I could barely think any further and I had little energy left to read. Moreover, I was so mentally exhausted that I couldn't digest any more of the information I was reading. So, I went back over the information I had obtained, in just more than two years of research. I had also been working double and triple duty for two years, working on both my *Stories From Maine* Facebook page, and preparing to write my second volume of *Stories From Maine*. I was also making videos of episodes of my *Stories From Maine* pilot season for YouTube. To say I was at my breaking point would be an understatement. I needed to get away and have a breather so I took a ride down to the waterfront in Portland. But, no matter how tired I may have been, history was never far from my thoughts.

I enjoyed the warm sunshine as it shone down upon my face, much as Joseph Drew did as he walked to the gallows, not far from where I was standing. I stood at the edge of the water and thought in depth about the history that had taken place there in Portland. I thought of the men of the United States Navy – during World War Two - as they boarded the USS Eagle 56 for the last time. They had walked right where I was now standing, there at the docks before me, on April 23rd of 1945. Hours later their boat was torpedoed by German Submarine U-853 just off the Coast of Cape Elizabeth. I thought of the Great Fire of 1866 that burned and ravaged the city behind me, a fire which is believed to have destroyed many of the records that I now struggled to locate. I thought of the insanity and sadness of the bombing of Falmouth in October of 1775 by the five British Warships under the command of Lieutenant Henry Mowatt. The cannons of these warships targeted that old colonial city on the hill from the harbor, which I now looked out at. And, I thought of John and Ebenezer Parker as they crouched at the ready behind a wall at Fort Hancock, in Cape Elizabeth, ready to defend their homeland from enemy invaders. From where I stood, I could see the site of old Fort Hancock as well. I then turned back and looked up India Street to the corner where Dr. Coffin's house once stood, and I then turned around to look at where the ferry had once docked at the wharf, right at the end of that street in 1808. I then looked over,

175.

across the harbor, to what was then the Cape Elizabeth shore. I could see the modern-day restaurant where Joseph Parker's ferry once docked. I could also see the steeple of the modern Congregational Church, straight up the hill from that restaurant, and I thought of Joseph and Elisha Parker building the very first of these churches in 1734.

Then something dawned on me, something that had occurred to me before, but I had not focused on. Although I could not find Ebenezer, I also could not find his father Nathaniel. And, I also could not find Ebenezer's Grandfather Joseph either.

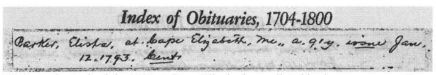

Elisha Parker's death in 1791 at Cape Elizabeth was listed in the newspapers. But, his grave also could not be located.

Nor could I find Ebenezer's Uncle Elisha. I could also not find Ebenezer's mother Hannah, Aunt Esther, or the man I called Uncle Ebenezer (Captain Ebenezer Parker). In fact, I could not locate between eight and eleven of these Parkers. And, of these missing Parkers, one thing was now clear to me, they all had a few things in common. First, they were all members of Deputy Parker's immediate family. Secondly, they all had strong ties to, or had lived in, Cape Elizabeth. And, they each had strong ties to that church, there on the hill, the one whose steeple I was now staring at. How was it possible that I could find all of the Parkers, be they in Standish, Gorham, Durham, Bridgton, Westbrook, Portland,

Falmouth, Cumberland, Yarmouth, or Freeport, and even in Brunswick, but I could not find these Parkers of Cape Elizabeth? How did all of these other Parker graves survive the test of time, except for these eight to eleven? By now I was standing at the edge of the Maine State Pier and staring off across the harbor to what was then the shore of Cape Elizabeth in 1808.

All of what I had found now faded to the back of my brain, while everything I could not find was now flooding through my mind. One thing became crystal clear to me: I needed to look once again at the last cemetery on my list, the one I could not confirm nor eliminate. It was painfully clear to me that I had to return to Cape Elizabeth.

Chapter Sixteen

Once found, the reclaimed Stackpole pages changed everything.

The Smoking Gun

By the summer of 2021, a new administration and staff were in place at the Westbrook Historical Society, and I had been conversing with Mark Swett on a mystery surrounding a dump in Westbrook and the 1937 case of a missing South Portland woman. I asked Mark if he could look around the society archives and see if there was anything he could find on Deputy Ebenezer Parker, Joseph Drew, or the assault at Saccarappa in January of 1808. His reply was, "I think I just saw a file laying around here somewhere with

Parker's name on it!" BINGO! The file Mark discovered was filled with a great many handwritten notes from someone who had been making their own attempt to locate the grave of Deputy Ebenezer Parker. Within a week, or so, Mark was able to scan and email all of the contents of a file for my perusal. For hours, I scoured and read each note, and I could see the researcher had covered a lot of the same ground I had also covered in the early days of the Inquiry. By now, I knew what was true and I recognized rumor, falsehood, and confused information that had once stumped my efforts as well. Then, I opened a scanned file of four, old, typewritten pages and I

began to read each with piqued curiosity. I immediately knew the validity of the information, and I recognized the writing style of author and historian Everett S. Stackpole.

At the very beginning of the Inquiry, it was Stackpole's *History of Durham*, which was one of the most contributing factors to the confusion surrounding the Parker mystery. Stackpole's enumeration of the John Parker family at Durham was a jumble of confused names, dates, and facts surrounding the family of Deputy Parker's brother John and his wife Elizabeth Warren Parker. The book was published in 1899 and by 1903, William McLellan's *History of Gorham* had been published. McLellan's book enumerated the names, dates, and facts surrounding the Parker family of Nathaniel and Hannah

Roberts Parker, John, and Ebenezer's parents. I knew by 2021 just how sound the information was in the *History of Gorham*, and just how inaccurate the pertinent information was in the *History of Durham*. Even Stackpole, in these four re-discovered pages, admitted to his mistakes in his book. Stackpole then attempted to correct the record. It is impossible to tell if he was planning to re-publish a second volume of the *History of Durham* or just place his corrections on file, but he was definitely attempting to correct his mistakes and salvage his work and his reputation as a pre-eminent historian.

Stackpole wrote about Joseph and Elisha Parker and their coming to Cape Elizabeth. He wrote about their lands and their family. He covered about as much as could be covered, and he made two personal visits to Cape Elizabeth to thoroughly ensure, and personally check his final accuracy. As I read the pages I recognized every bit of the information he wrote about. I already knew about the lands, the ferry boat, and the canoes, Joseph had owned and sold to his son. I knew of the Parker family and I recognized that what Stackpole was now correcting in this rewrite was accurate. Then, I came across a new bit of information not previously known nor published in Stackpole's earlier work. Suddenly I read the words, "I have twice examined the old cemetery and found the long Parker lot, where there are only small field stones not inscribed." I was floored! I was astonished. Finally, some mention of where the Parkers were buried had been located. And, in his 19th-century way of writing, Stackpole enumerated the family and told us, to a larger extent, who was in that cemetery. Yet his descriptions did not mention the cemetery by its exact name, nor did he tell us exactly where the "long Parker lot" was located. And, for as much as my excitement was elevated, and my curiosity piqued, I had some questions; the first was "How did he know these were our Parkers?"

I have twice examined the old cemetery — and found the long Parker lot, where there are only small field stones, not inscribed,

An edited excerpt from the "Stackpole Pages."

I was stunned by the revelation in the Stackpole pages. It might certainly be the most important discovery thus far, in the long and laborious quest of the Parker Inquiry. Yet, Stackpole had already left a bad taste in my mouth with *the History of Durham,* back in the initial research stages of the Inquiry, and his credit with me at this point was a little shaky. I had wasted a lot of time chasing down information based on his Durham-Parker genealogy and I was not interested in taking another ride on a Stackpole Merry-Go-Round to nowhere. For as much as the statement he made, in the description of the Cape Elizabeth cemetery, had made me smile, it also made me leery. How did he know these were our Parkers if it is a long line of graves "where there are only small field stones not inscribed?" He wrote in the document that no records for the burials in the cemetery existed, as church records had been destroyed in a fire. I knew the records were destroyed in a fire, as Stackpole admitted, and he mentioned no other records leading him to conclude that the graves he had "twice examined" were indeed our Parkers of Cape Elizabeth.

So, again, I had to know, how was it that he knew this to be true? Throughout the entirety of this inquiry, whenever I found myself stumped by some seemingly-unanswerable question or some confusion of information, I generally discovered that genealogy would help to sort out the confusion and provide the answers I needed. After reading these Stackpole pages over and over, searching for some clues - and praying for some clear realization - which might allow me to believe in his information, I decided I now had to research Everett Stackpole himself.

I sat down and began a reverse research of the man, of his life and career, from his death backward. I noted his books and the subjects which he wrote about, and I noted his lineage and his ancestors. However, nothing stood out as being noteworthy. Then, I went back to the start, Stackpole's childhood, and worked sideways – a parallel search of genealogy – to discover just who his extended family was. I wanted to know who he knew, and who he worked with or was related to. I wanted to know where he lived and who his neighbors were. And, I planned to continue looking until I found some connection, some reasonable explanation, or some kind of plausibility which could help me to understand how he could know who was buried in what he called "the long Parker lot." Fortunately, I didn't have to search for very long. It was a very short process before I realized that Everett's sister Sarah had married Gardner Larrabee, and I already knew that Gardner Larrabee was the grandson of Deputy Parker's sister Anna Parker Larrabee. And, then it occurred to me that the old cemetery in Durham, where many of the Durham Parkers and Larrabees are buried – near to where the three Parker/Larrabee farms stood – was located along the Stackpole Road. I now realized just how Everett Stackpole knew that "the long Parker lot" was indeed a long lot of our Cape Elizabeth Parker graves. Everett Stackpole was a member of the family.

Stackpole must have had access to family documents, maybe handwritten maps, or a family bible. He obviously had access to his brother-in-law and was able to discuss the family with him, and with other family members. Stackpole was a true historian and he was used to accumulating oral histories and documents to weave a history together. Stackpole was also out to correct his past mistake, one that would eat at him and would drive most true historians a little nuts. Stackpole was looking to correct the record and repair the integrity of his work and his reputation. He was out to restore his self-esteem, and leaving an incorrect genealogy of his own family, albeit an extended one, was simply unacceptable. And, in Stackpole's description of the cemetery, he referenced "a Sexton or Caretaker." This leaves me to wonder if this keeper of the cemetery may also have led Everett to the graves of the Parkers of Cape Elizabeth. I now had little reason to doubt the veracity of the written conclusions of Everett Stackpole. And, this fit with everything I already knew about the Parker family.

In the end consideration of Stackpole's pages, the fit into my own research was perfect. I had performed extensive genealogies of the Parker family and their extended clan. I had scoured cemeteries all through Cumberland County in those first three years of the

Inquiry and I had located all of Deputy Parker's immediate family, and most of the closer and extended relations as well. I knew where everyone was, that is except for up to eleven Parkers - and all of those eleven Parkers were the Parkers of Cape Elizabeth - including Deputy Parker himself. And, here was Stackpole writing about these Parkers, and he was telling me they were in this cemetery. As far as the Historian's Inquiry into finding the final resting place of murdered Cumberland County Deputy Sheriff Ebenezer Parker was concerned, the Stackpole pages were a "smoking gun."

Furthermore, the discovery of these pages had helped Jim Rowe at the Cape Elizabeth Historical Preservation Society to go back and dig some more in their archives. He had soon discovered that the Society did have copies of the Stackpole pages. As far as I was able to ascertain, the Cape Elizabeth archive was Stackpole's repository for his corrections. And, as it turned out, a descendant of John Parker – Judy Parker Cole - also on her own hunt for Parker family genealogy had discovered those pages some years previous to my discovery. She had re-transcribed these early 20th-century pages into a modern Word document and left the transcription with the Society. She also had the presence of mind to leave her contact information on the new transcription. I soon found myself talking to Judy Parker Cole, a direct descendent of Deputy Parker's brother, John Parker. Judy was living in Massachusetts, and we were able to compare notes. I did not doubt that these Stackpole pages were genuine and that Stackpole was trying to correct the record he had created and put the corrected information into the hands of future historians and genealogists by leaving these four pages of his findings with the Cape Elizabeth archive. I now had lots of reason to believe these Parkers, my 8 to 11 Parkers of Cape Elizabeth, were interred at the Mount Pleasant Cemetery, in what is now South Portland, Maine. But, my belief was not going to be nearly enough. At the same time as I was exploring the veracity of the Stackpole pages I was also continuing the search for other documents and proof to back up Stackpole's assertions. And, if Deputy Parker was, as I now theorized, one of the "Parker 11" at Mount Pleasant, I would need to have more than just my own translation of Stackpole's report, I needed more supportive evidence. And, I was still searching for more details from one of the men who, by his telling, had been at the funeral of Deputy Ebenezer Parker.

Reverend Caleb Bradley had been an instrumental figure from the very start of the Parker Inquiry. He was a man who loomed large in the early days of Stroudwater, Saccarappa, and Falmouth Neck. And, as it turned out, he was also instrumental in a small period of Cape Elizabeth's history as well. Bradley had spent a great deal of time with Joseph Drew, and the old curmudgeon of a minister was also neck-deep in the hanging of Deputy Parker's killer. He was involved enough with Deputy Parker's widow that she apparently saw fit to name her newborn son Caleb after the old Parson. And, Bradley's name kept coming up in nearly everything else I had researched. Over and over again, the name Caleb Bradley resurfaced consistently concerning the Parker Inquiry and I knew that he had "attended" Deputy Parker's funeral. But, how did "attending" to Parker's funeral help back up the Stackpole findings? I needed more information. I had begun corresponding with the  Congregational Church at Woodford's Corner, now Portland, which had been begun by Bradley. I was looking for more of his records and letters. They told me they had a room full of records and documents, photographs, and other items, all of which they had not yet cataloged. They allowed me access to these materials and I spent an afternoon going through each document and every item in this collection. Unfortunately, nothing was found to be of much help.

I was also corresponding with the Congregational Church Archives in Massachusetts. Archivist William McCarthy was able to verify a lot of information that I had only some slight reference to. It seemed that the Congregational Minister William Gregg, the minister who had married Ebenezer Parker to Mary Larrabee at Cape Elizabeth in 1805, had left the Cape Elizabeth church in 1806. However, the church elders had not found a replacement for Gregg, and Caleb Bradley had volunteered for double duty. Not only would Reverend Bradley continue as the Pastor of the Stroudwater Congregational Church, which covered Saccarappa as well as Stroudwater, but he also began covering the Cape Elizabeth Parish while the members conducted a long and drawn-out search for a new and permanent pastor. And, McCarthy was able to confirm that

186.

Bradley held this position from 1806 until a new replacement was installed in 1809.

The Church that Bradley was now covering in Cape Elizabeth was the exact one built by Joseph and Elisha Parker and that church was built in the old cemetery on Meeting House Hill. And, Bradley would have been covering as Pastor of the Cape Elizabeth Congregational Church on January 18th of 1808, and most especially on January 20th of 1808, when Bradley "attended" to the funeral of Deputy Ebenezer Parker "the man killed by Drew at Saccarappa." If any doubt still lingered in my mind as to the veracity of the findings that Everett Stackpole had left to posterity - in his old typed pages – then it was the Caleb Bradley connection and the history of the Congregational Church which had just laid them to rest. It was now time to find the "long Parker lot."

Chapter Seventeen

Image of Mount Pleasant Cemetery taken somewhere between 1834 and 1899. Photo Courtesy of the Maine Historical Society.

Another Process of Elimination

By the time Stackpole had "twice visited" the Cape Elizabeth cemetery, where he described the "long Parker lot," the cemetery itself had already undergone a lot of changes since Deputy Parker died in 1808. What had been the Northern District of Maine in the Commonwealth of Massachusetts was now the State of Maine. The old cemetery in Cape Elizabeth that Stackpole had described was now named the Mount Pleasant Cemetery, and this portion of Cape Elizabeth was now – since 1895 – the City of South Portland. The Parkers of Cape Elizabeth were now gone from the town and even the original church that Joseph and Elisha had built was replaced by a newer church, built in the same spot inside the cemetery, in 1834. And, even that church was later dismantled and a new church was built across the street. Within four decades of the last Parker burial, the Mount Pleasant Cemetery would also see further dramatic changes as a group of ladies of Cape Elizabeth had gathered, formed a board of trustees for the cemetery, and planned improvements. Expansion of the old graveyard, clearing of vines that had overtaken tombstones, thickets of tall grass, brush, wild growing trees, and an installation of a fence around the property, were all begun by 1874. And, these ladies also sought to tackle another problem that was common to old cemeteries; they intended to level off the uneven and trough-ridden cemetery. It was a massive undertaking, and

one that required a great many hands, and a lot of planning. What Stackpole was seeing between the years of 1903 and 1927 was a drastic difference from what the cemetery looked like at the time of the last Parker death – and probable Cape Elizabeth burial – in 1833. Since Stackpole's visit, even more changes had occurred to the old cemetery upon Meeting House Hill. It was now a much larger cemetery than it had ever been and a great community of homes and businesses had arisen around it, not to mention the creation of paved roads, concrete walkways, and the passing of a great many decades of changes due to weather.

By 1938, the United States was still imbued in the latest economic depression, this time it was called "Hoover's Depression" or the Great Depression, and it had already lasted for nine years. President Franklin Delano Roosevelt had already initiated a great deal of programs to deal with the financial hardships of the Great Depression, in an effort to put all areas and sectors of the American workforce back to gainful work. One of the alphabet agencies created to oversee such works programs was the Works Progress Administration (WPA). And, one of the programs or tasks of the WPA was to provide preservation, mapping, and transcription of the names of the dead who were buried in old cemeteries, and to record the names of America's veterans, especially those of the American Revolution.

By the time the WPA had arrived in South Portland, their system had been well-tested and worked with ease, like a well-oiled machine. It had become an automatic process for this eclectic group of historians, writers, architects, surveyors, cartographers, archaeologists, and genealogists, to name a few. The surveyors and cartographers set out to design a grid and map out the Mount Pleasant Cemetery into numbered sections with numerical lots. Architects then added the information to a scaled drawing of the cemetery, thereby creating a formal blueprint of the graveyard. Meanwhile, the historians and genealogists of the endeavor descended upon the area libraries and historical societies, the town

190.

and city offices, and began scouring old directories, tax rolls, death records, newspaper obituaries, and books on local history, in order to find records of burials which no longer had stone-cold evidence standing within the cemetery boundaries. The work of the WPA was the most thorough and ambitious endeavor carried out at Mount Pleasant Cemetery since a group of ladies had labored to clean up the old and neglected graveyard nearly sixty-five years earlier. The WPA had a huge endeavor ahead of them, to map and transcribe the Mount Pleasant Cemetery, but a new and threatening storm of war in Europe was threatening to bring the work to an abrupt halt.

The lower, left, corner label of the WPA blueprint for Mount Pleasant cemetery. Courtesy of the South Portland Historical Society, Online.

The results of the work of the WPA seemed a promising and ironic discovery. It seemed likely that whatever Stackpole had seen when he "twice visited" Mount Pleasant Cemetery, must have been found by this massive undertaking of research and documentation of the graveyard. After all, the WPA was accumulating facts and information, data, and creating a scientific mapping of the cemetery, complete with historical and genealogical evidence. Any proof that the Parkers were here should have been recorded as a result of the WPA's efforts. It was also ironic that the WPA was an effort for an economic solution to the Great Depression since it was a great economic depression in 1807 which was, at the root, a cause of Deputy Parker's death. The Inquiry quickly focused on trying to locate the records, and most especially the notes, of the WPA team who worked at Mount Pleasant Cemetery. Emails were immediately sent to a contact at the Library of Congress (LOC) in Washington, the Maine Historical Society (MHS) in Portland, the Maine State Archives (MSA) in Augusta, and the National Archives and Records Administration (NARA) in Boston. But, after weeks of searching no record of an archive of notes or materials relating to the work of the WPA at Cape Elizabeth, other than the final results – which I already had – could be located. After three months of scouring records collections in Maine and within the Federal Government, it seemed that all I had was all I would find.

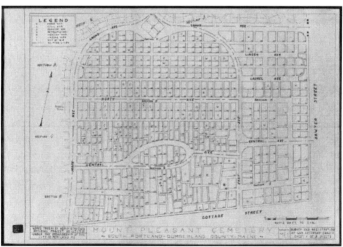

1 of 3 pages of the WPA blueprint. Courtesy of the South Portland Historical Society, online.

After all the work the WPA had done, after all the research and all the examination and mapping of the cemetery that they had accomplished, there was no mention of the Parkers of Cape Elizabeth.

Town records in both Falmouth and South Portland had been examined and the Parkers were indeed present within the original records books that are safeguarded by the town and city clerks. Original entries of marriages, births, and deaths, of our Parkers of Cape Elizabeth, had been located in these ledgers. However, no mention of where any of the Parker 8 to 11 had been buried could be found. Numerous newspapers of the 1700s, and early 1800s, were re-scoured as well for obituaries or the then-called "Death Notices." Some were located, and many were not. The census information could only help with a limited range of years. The first Decennial Census in America was conducted in 1790 and took place, as it still does every ten years.

By 1790, three of our Parker 11, Prudence, Joseph, and Nathaniel, had already died. Two of the 11, Deputy Parker and his mother Hannah, were still living in Gorham. 1 of the 11, Benjamin Fickett, had not even entered the Parker picture as of yet. And, only four of our Parker 11 were alive and living in Cape Elizabeth. By the 1800 census, one of the Parker 11, Elisha Parker, in Cape Elizabeth had already died. And, by the census of 1810, both Esther Parker and Deputy Parker were now dead and buried, and Esther's husband Captain Ebenezer Parker had gone to live with his son Eleazer at Standish. The Inquiry was able to discern who died, and when, and could tell where these Parkers had died. However, nothing was located that gave any indication as to where any of the Parker 11 had been buried. All the Inquiry had to go by were the four Stackpole pages.

For as much as the Stackpole pages appeared brutally clear to some they left many others shaking their head. Stackpole went into a great deal of detail when it came to describing some of the early Parkers of Cape Elizabeth, and their immediate line of descendants. He described the lands, the relationships, and the documents he found, as well as the records that could not be found. The relationship between what he was describing and the Mount Pleasant Cemetery was hard to deny. Yet, Stackpole did not call the cemetery by name and he did not describe where he found the "long Parker lot" to be "well situated." Yet, up to 11 Parkers of Cape Elizabeth were missing, and since all other Parkers had been identified and located - in cemeteries throughout Cumberland and a few portions of Androscoggin Counties – then the identification of these Parkers in the "long Parker lot" appeared quite obvious. If all the Parkers had been identified and located, except for these 11 Parkers of Cape Elizabeth, then Stackpole had to be referring to these, the Parker 11. If he was not, then who could he have been referring to when all others had been located? It seemed a surety that the "long Parker lot" had to be a space that could accommodate between 8 and 11 Parkers. And, it was obvious that the "small field stones not inscribed," which Stackpole identified in his pages, were apparently no longer able to be seen above the soil. Thus, it was logical that the Inquiry was looking for a swath of ground in the cemetery that appeared to have no burials and no markers.

The Inquiry began to focus on examining the cemetery using the transcription of names, and the survey map of the WPA, as well as overhead imagery and mapping via Google Earth. First, it was also logical to assume that the section naming of the cemetery, assigned by the WPA, was not done in chronological order. Since the earliest Parker burial that could be ascertained was that of Prudence Atwood Parker – first wife of Elisha – in 1748, then in the original section of the cemetery, the oldest part, would have been the first in the "long Parker lot," assuming they were all buried together. The area now labeled as "Section-G" was quickly identified to be the majority of the oldest part of the original cemetery and it would have stood alongside the original church that Joseph and Elisha Parker had built. The next Parker burial would not have been for twenty-six years, with Joseph Parker's passing in 1774. That would have been followed fifteen years later by the burial of Joseph's son Nathaniel, Deputy Parker's father, in 1789. Then, Joseph's brother Elisha followed in 1793. And, since the first stone cutter is not known to have come to the Falmouth Neck area until Bartlett Adams arrived in about 1800, it is likely that these four-first Parker burials only received "small field stones not inscribed," common for many during the time. It seemed logical that the original Parkers who settled in Cape Elizabeth, who built the church in the graveyard and owned much of the land around the cemetery, were buried in the oldest, original, section of that graveyard. And, since the first of the Parker 8-11 burials took place nearly two-hundred and seventy-five years earlier, it seemed acceptable that evidence of some of these burials had disappeared from detection.

When Section G was viewed using Google Earth one thing was glaringly clear. There was a ninety-foot swath of open land with only three standing headstones. When the transcription of names was examined and the known burials were compared to the survey map, one other thing also became clear; there was an obvious lack of names denoting known burials for this open swath of the cemetery. And, when the Google Earth Imagery was applied to the WPA survey map the swath of open cemetery land now had identifying labels. The WPA survey showed five "long lots" that ran from the edge of the cemetery, inward into Section G. These lots were identified as lots #43, 44, 45, 46, and 47. It seemed likely that if the Parker 8-11 were buried in what Stackpole had described as the "long Parker lot" then these five lots could be where the Parkers of Cape Elizabeth were buried.

More information had to be found. There had to be a direct connection or some sort of record, something that would indicate that this long swath of ground could hold the remains of Cape Elizabeth's 8-11 Parkers. However, there were no church records or town records, and no death records or obituaries to help link these Parkers to these identified lots. All the Inquiry had to go on was a transcription list of known burials and the headstones which still stood in the long swath of Section G. At the far end of the swath, in lot #47, was the 1826 burial of Jane H. Bradbury. A genealogical study revealed that Jane was originally Jane H. Brackett of Portland,

196.

who had married Charles Bradbury of Cape Elizabeth, in 1825. Nine months after their marriage Jane died in what may have been childbirth. Her husband, who died many years later, was buried in the Eastern Cemetery in Portland, but Jane was all alone in Cape Elizabeth. I could find no relationship between the Bracketts or the Bradburys and the Parkers of Cape Elizabeth. At the opposite end of the swath was another lone-standing stone belonging to "little Glennie Sewall" a young girl who died far before her time. I could also find no connection between little Glennie and our Parker 11. It seemed we were striking out.

Yet, in the middle of the long swath stands another lone stone, this one belongs to the wife of George W. Miller a man who died in Hawaii in about 1851. When the transcription list of these lots was examined it yielded two more names for G-Section Lot #46 as those of Peter and Elizabeth Miller, who died in 1827 and 1826 respectively. Although no stone remained for Peter and Elizabeth their names had been placed on the transcription list as occupants of lot #46. It was time to perform another genealogical search, only this time the research would be on Peter and Elizabeth Miller. When the study was complete the Inquiry had a connection to the Parker family. As it turned out, Elizabeth Miller was in actuality Elizabeth Parker Miller, and she was the daughter of Captain Ebenezer Parker and his wife Esther Higgins Parker. And, George Miller was the son or grandson of this Peter and Elizabeth. And, the extended Miller family was also buried in the long lot of graves next to this long swath of ground. It appeared likely, and it was quite logical, that if

197.

there was a "long Parker lot" in the Mount Pleasant Cemetery, as Stackpole had described, they would be buried in the original section of the cemetery, in a swath of land where it seemed that few graves existed, where a "long Parker lot" could exist, and where other family members were also buried, continuing the line. Section-G, lots #43-47 were now the prime target of the probability of the Historian's Inquiry into the location of the grave of Cumberland County Deputy Sheriff Ebenezer Parker.

Many remained unsold on the probability of this target being the "long Parker lot" that Stackpole described. In fact, a few still doubted that Stackpole was even referencing the Mount Pleasant Cemetery at all. Fortunately, Cumberland County Sheriff Kevin Joyce knew that the argument the Inquiry made for the likelihood of the "long Parker lot" being at Mount Pleasant Cemetery, and in the long swath of probable lots, had merit. But, how could any of this be determined to be accurate? How could anyone know for a fact there were other graves in this seemingly vacant swath of graveyard? And, how would this information help to yield evidence of the presence of a grave belonging to Deputy Ebenezer Parker? There was only one way to proceed and it would require obtaining the permission of the Mount Pleasant Cemetery Board of Trustees.

Sheriff Joyce began talks with members of the Board of Trustees and he began arranging for a scientific solution to the quandary of how to proceed. We had the possible location of almost a dozen, nearly three-hundred-year-old, graves with only the word and logic determined by one historian to base a further examination of the cemetery. A meeting was scheduled for October 27th of 2022, to be held in the cemetery between the Sherriff, the trustees, and myself, making the case. Jim Rowe, from the Cape Elizabeth Historical Preservation Society, was also present for the meeting as I told the tale and laid out my theories, and my evidence. I did my best to tell it all, to show them what I could see and what I knew to be true. This was the last cemetery to be searched, there were no more left with any reason to be looked at with any seriousness. And, so far, this cemetery had the best likelihood of being the resting place of the Parkers of Cape Elizabeth then had any of the other cemeteries that had been considered or searched, and finally eliminated.

When the meeting was over, the present members of the Mount Pleasant Cemetery were willing to proceed. Sheriff Joyce was eager to move forward in this, the case he had worked for two decades to solve. And, the Sheriff had found a way to determine if there were any graves whatsoever in this long swath of land, this proposed "long Parker lot." Sheriff Joyce and one of his detectives, Brian Ackerman, had located a Geophysicist in New Hampshire who was happy to donate his time and resources to help. Science was about to enter the Inquiry and either support historical theory or obliterate it. The Geophysicist was bringing in a very sensitive and very expensive piece of equipment to Mount Pleasant Cemetery, and the Board of Trustees had voted to approve its use. It would just be another month and then the rubber would meet the road, and science would come to bear. The Geophysicist was bringing in Ground Penetrating Radar, which could read deep into the ground and tell us if there were, or were not, any graves actually present in this potential "long Parker lot." It seemed that both the conclusion of Everett Stackpole and the theoretical determination of the Historian's Inquiry were now about to stand a trial by fire.

Chapter Eighteen

Peter Leach of Geophysical Survey Systems Inc, of Nashua New Hampshire, prepares to begin a ground penetrating radar scan of the long Parker lot on December 2nd, 2022. Photo courtesy of the author.

Probing The Long Parker Lot.

On December 2nd of 2022, my nerves were beginning to fray at their ends. I was tired, both mentally and physically, and I felt the time constraints of the impending winter, which was fast approaching. Everything I had worked for over the last four years was about to be tested to the limits of my conclusions. My theory of the location of Stackpole's "Long Parker Lot" was about to be examined by modern-day scientific methods. And, although Sheriff Joyce had limited the number of participants and spectators who would be there, several people were still expected to be at the cemetery for the scanning. My reputation as a historian was on the line, and by the end of the day, we would have some firm idea if the proposed "Long Parker Lot" location was indeed a lost burial plot or just an open and vacant patch of ground. We would also know if any of my conclusions had any veracity at all, or if all that I had worked for was completely unfounded.

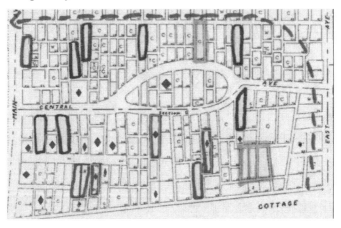

An examination of all long lots helped to narrow down and eliminate many possible locations. A working map of the inquiry.

My theory of where the "Long Parker Lot" was located seemed to perplex many people. Either they didn't see the likelihood, didn't agree with my conclusions, or just didn't understand what exactly it was that I knew. I felt I had a thorough picture in my mind of the early days of Cape Elizabeth, of the building of the church, the people who lived there, the community itself, and how the Mount Pleasant Cemetery originally came together. And, I felt I had a thorough idea of just how the Parker family fit into this whole overall picture. In my mind, my choice of the probable location of Stackpole's "Long Parker Lot" made complete and utter sense. Yet, not many others seemed to agree with my theory. Fortunately, Sheriff Kevin Joyce felt my argument had merit and, from an investigator's standpoint, all possibilities still had to be checked out. I had felt that all which I could do, as a historian, had been done. Now, I pointed to a piece of open ground and turned everything over to the Sheriff. The rest was up to him. Through many professional contacts, Sheriff Joyce was able to locate a Geophysicist who was happy to join the search and one who would donate his time. Cumberland County Detective Brian Ackerman had made the connection with the Geophysicist possible and had arranged for a scan of the cemetery, at the "Long Parker Lot." Sheriff Joyce had been in communication with members of the Board of Trustees of the Mount Pleasant Cemetery and he asked for permission for the team to perform the scan. This had required the Sheriff, and myself to meet with the Trustees at the cemetery in November and present our case. When our presentation was over they happily agreed to allow the Sheriff to perform the non-invasive scan. Now, with everything in place, the day of the Ground Penetrating Radar scan had arrived. And, by the end of the day, I would either be supported by the scientific results, or I would be the laughable, 21st Century version of Geraldo Rivera and his humiliating search for the Tombs of Al Capone.

The "long Parker lot."

Mount Pleasant Cemetery, G-Section, lots #43-#47. This is the proposed "long Parker lot." The headstone in the upper center belongs to the wife of George W. Miller. Image courtesy of the Author.

My reputation as a historian was on the line. But, the strange part of the day, at least for me, was that I was no longer a participant or driving force in the Inquiry. I wasn't even a part of the team at all. I was now just a spectator, and my fate as a historian hinged on the results of the scan.

204.

When I arrived at Mount Pleasant Cemetery, at about nine that morning, several people had already arrived before me. Sheriff Joyce and Deputy Detective Brian Ackerman were already on site. So too were a number of the cemetery's Trustees, as well as Mark Swett of the Westbrook Historical Society, and Jim Rowe of the Cape Elizabeth Historical Preservation Society. And, already setting up his equipment was Peter Leach of Geophysical Survey Systems who traveled up from Nashua, in New Hampshire, to donate his time to help us find the final resting place of Deputy Ebenezer Parker. It was not a great start for me, as it turned out, I was the last to arrive. I was late to an event that I, my efforts, my conclusions, and at my behest, was the sole reason for taking place at all. Peter was already setting up a very sensitive and technical piece of machinery known as Ground Penetrating Radar (GPR). This sort of apparatus looks similar to a high-tech, electric, or solar lawn mower, with a tall Global Positioning Satellite (GPS) Receiver mounted upon it. And, it has a monitor screen perched upon the handlebars, which allows a graphic-style digital image of the data being received by the GPR scanner, which hovers just fractions of an inch about the ground. Peter took the time to explain to all of us what his machine did, what he would be doing, and what sort of data he would be assessing. He was patient, and he even allowed many of us to try out the machine, then he explained the data that we had collected. When the demonstration was complete we all had a fair layperson's understanding of the very complicated and technical process that was about to take place. Then, Peter got down to a very slow, very methodical, quite exacting, process of work.

A few hours had passed as Peter wheeled his machined back and forth in parallel paths, each overlapping the other, from one end of the "Long Parker Lot," ninety feet or so toward the fence line, then back again. From the edge of one long line of standing stones, approximately twenty feet across to the other, Peter continued to slowly roll the GPR over every inch of the ground while the deep penetrating radar bounced signal after signal down into the cold earth, then received back those hot signals and recorded the data from just below.

The ground penetrating radar unit, over the "long Parker lot" at Mount Pleasant Cemetery on December 2, 2022. Photo courtesy of the Author.

Now and again, Peter would stop, take notes and measurements, and then continue on. When Peter had finally come into the area of the "Long Parker Lot," where I had theorized broken headstones would most likely be laid down under the soil, he looked for any data on his screen that might support that theory. I was talking with the Sheriff when Mark Swett called me over. Mark was on his knees with a thin metal probe in his hand and he had told me that Peter just noted a possible stone was present. Mark sunk the probe and in just a few inches the probe was met with a solid, stone-like, thunk. He pulled the probe, reset it just an inch away, and tried again. Thunk! He reset it again and again. Thunk! Thunk! Mark looked up at me and said "Lori, that's a stone!"

Mark Swett of the Westbrook Historical Society sinks a small hand probe and hits what could be a fallen headstone just beneath the surface of the soil in the "long Parker lot." Photo courtesy of the Author.

Within the next half an hour Mark had discovered the location of nearly half a dozen hand-probed stones that were lying just under the surface. Soon, Peter had been over enough of the "Long Parker Lot" to form an unofficial field diagnosis opinion. I asked, "Do you see anything here in this long lot that indicates graves?" Peter stopped what he was doing, turned back and pointed toward the fence line, and said, "I can see what appear to be three or four on that end." Then Peter turned back and pointed to the other end of the "Long Parker Lot" and explained, "…and what seems to be another three or four at this end."

I finally felt a moment of relief that I had not felt all day. I finally felt my shoulders loosen, and my abdominal muscles relax.

Suddenly I took in a breath and began to breathe again. Although Peter's field opinion was, as he cautioned, not scientific evidence it was enough to tell me that my theory about burials being in this location was correct. And, that my theories about a catastrophic event taking down standing headstones, might also have been correct. And, the indicator that stones indeed appeared to be present told me that this entire endeavor to locate the final resting place of Deputy Ebenezer Parker was still far from over. If these were indeed graves that Peter's GPR was indicating, as being deep under the soil in the "Long Parker Lot," and if the stones that Mark's probing had located could be unearthed, we might still have an opportunity to find a headstone with the name "Ebenezer Parker" engraved upon it. But, for now, I could only take some solace in the knowledge that we did not come up empty-handed, that even if these graves were not our Parkers of Cape Elizabeth, they were still people whose burials had been lost, and may now have been found. Fortunately, enough information had been scientifically determined to insure that the search for Deputy Ebenezer Parker could indeed continue.

Of course, we had to wait for the official results of the scan before anyone could discuss the next steps. But, there were now new options to be considered. First, since these probable headstone possibilities could be re-located with absolute exactness, by the results of the GPR scan, then these fallen stones could be unearthed with minimal excavation, and the ground could be easily repaired with minimal cost or effort. Then, the stones could be identified – if any legible identifying print was discerned – and the stones could be replaced above their proper grave. However, the repair and reinstallation of these stones could be costly. That raises the question of who would pay the cost of that work. Second, a decision might be made to leave the stones in place, where they are, and leave the graves completely undisturbed. In this case, there would be no way to ever identify those buried in the graves of the "Long Parker Lot." Should the second option be chosen, then the grave of Deputy Ebenezer Parker might never be identified. In the second case option, a stone might be placed at the head of the "Long Parker Lot" identifying it as a possible location of the grave of Deputy Ebenezer Parker. Either way, the GPR scan of the "Long Parker Lot," and the unofficial diagnosis opinion – should it match the final results – leave questions to be discussed and answers to be decided. And, if the first option – to unearth the stones – is decided to be the next step in the process it would be some months before that step would likely begin. Winter was now setting in, the ground was beginning to freeze, and any planned unearthing of headstones – should the decision to do so be made – would now have to wait until spring.

Christmas 2022 was quickly approaching, and verbal delivery of the day's unofficial field results was an early and welcome gift to the many Parker descendants who I have kept in contact with on my Facebook page. Many finally had the opportunity to know if the grave of their fourth or fifth great-grandfather or great-uncle – Deputy Ebenezer Parker – might be closer to being found. Each quickly asked many questions, and each wanted to know when the final results would arrive, and what the next steps would be. I had provided video and photographs from the cemetery, and the events that had taken place throughout the day, and I posted commentary and updates continually, as I knew that many were eagerly monitoring my page for updates. These descendants of Mary Larrabee and Ebenezer Parker, and even John and Elizabeth Warren Parker, had been following my trek through the mystery of the search for Ebenezer Parker's final resting place for years and many were even more excited for the arrival of this day than I was. Fortunately, the preliminary news was good enough to bring a smile to every one of the Parker descendants.

With this part of the Inquiry completed, and with my work seemingly finished, there was only one thing left for me to do. Since there were no more leads, no more places to look, no more documents that I could find, and no more theories to be explored – no matter what decision was made going forward at the cemetery – my Historian's Inquiry was completed. It was now time to sort through the mountain of information I had accumulated, put it all down into a narrative, and publish my findings. I was eager to get to work on writing the book and to get it all down in print while it was all still fresh in my mind, and while there was still air in my lungs. I had become overly concerned that the entire story of Deputy Parker, Joseph Drew, and Levi Quinby, and all of the true details of the event, lived only in my memory and within the reams of notes that were scattered upon my desk, within my computer, and in the pages of the notebooks I had kept for nearly five years. I was afraid that if something happened to me, then this entire story, and all of the supporting evidence and details, could once again become lost to history. It was now time for me to release the story and information I had gathered.

I immediately returned home from the cemetery and planned to take a week off to enjoy a bit of a mental break, enjoy the holidays, and start mentally preparing myself to write my fifth book. The pre-writing break also allowed time to receive the results of the cemetery scan and absorb the information that would, eventually, come from the scientific reading. And initially, we all expected that we might have the results of the GPR scan at Mount Pleasant Cemetery by Christmas, thus I planned to start the book right after the holidays were over. There was a lot of data that Peter had to go through, to transcribe and analyze. It would not be an easy job that faced this Geophysicist but it was one he was trained and experienced to handle. But, as it would turn out, our wait for an official report of the findings of the ground penetrating radar scan at Mount Pleasant Cemetery would take some months to receive and might likely not lead to any definitive answers for some time to come. I had followed all the information I could locate and, in the end, I was able to identify a likely location that could answer the original question of the Historian's Inquiry: Where is the final resting place of Cumberland County Deputy Sheriff Ebenezer Parker?

Epilogue

The murder of Cumberland County Deputy Sheriff Ebenezer Parker is one of the darkest and most nefarious events in Maine history. The lionization of Parker's killer as a hero to a beleaguered and downtrodden people was a complete bastardization of actuality and a complete miscarriage of reality. For more than two centuries a false myth was long perpetuated, one which continued to betray the truth and glorify the false. To this day, some 215 years later, the true story of the murder of Ebenezer Parker and the execution of Joseph Drew continues to be a story mired in false legend, and misrepresentation of facts, and it continues to put forth an unceasing belief that Deputy Parker was in the wrong when he sought out Levi Quinby on that fateful January day in 1808.

Although the murder of Ebenezer Parker and the trial and execution of Joseph Drew is often recalled, and the myth retold, the details are most often a blend of falsity and myth. For more than two centuries, the true details of these events have been long buried, hidden, misfiled, and mislaid to detection, and the true stories of these participants have defied discovery. With the conclusion of this Historian's Inquiry, the facts surrounding the life and death of Ebenezer Parker - once shrouded in confusion and mystery - have now been unearthed and thoroughly researched. Documents surrounding both Parker's murder and Drew's trial and execution were rediscovered in numerous state archives, historical and genealogical societies, libraries, Universities, church collections, old forgotten books, and in collections of archived newspapers, all kept in the many hidden locations of Maine, Massachusetts, Wisconsin, Minnesota, and elsewhere. For nearly five years the truth of who Deputy Ebenezer Parker was, who Joseph Drew was, and exactly what took place on January 11th of 1808, in Saccarappa (Westbrook), was pursued. Yet, discovering all of this information and discerning fact from fiction, truth from myth, all added to the overarching and original goal; to find the final resting place of Cumberland County Sheriff's Deputy Ebenezer Parker.

It had long been accepted that Deputy Parker was the first law enforcement officer to die in the line of duty in Maine's long and illustrious history. This historian's inquiry delved deeper into the known line-of-duty deaths of all law enforcement officers in Maine, Massachusetts, and New England and discovered that the truth was even more moving. For it soon became clear that while Maine was still a part of Massachusetts, as the Northern District of Maine, Deputy Ebenezer Parker was also the first law enforcement officer to die in Massachusetts history as well. Checking even further, it was discovered that Cumberland County Deputy Sheriff Ebenezer Parker was also the first law enforcement officer to die in the line of duty in all of New England history. And, of all the fallen officers in Maine's history, Deputy Ebenezer Parker was the only officer whose grave had not been located and whose graveside service and sacrifice could not be properly honored each Law Enforcement Officers Memorial Month.

The completion of the Historian's Inquiry into the murder and burial of Ebenezer Parker had quickly morphed from its simple beginning mission; to find the grave of Deputy Ebenezer Parker. Soon, the parameters of the search had expanded to discern and complete lengthy genealogies, discover locations of documents about the many people in the completed story, the trials, the events, etc. A boots-on-the-ground search of nearly a dozen cemeteries, examinations of nearly 120 newspapers from 1800-1835 were conducted, and hands-on searching of old church records, historical society holdings, and the archives of many libraries and Universities took place. What was initially thought to be a probable three-month project morphed into an in-depth and widespread historian's investigation lasting nearly five years.

In the end, the truth was discovered. Despite the lingering myth to the contrary, Deputy Ebenezer Parker was – according to the determination of the Supreme Judicial Court – acting within his duly authorized duty as a Deputy Sheriff of Cumberland County, when he and his posse of men, tracked Levi Quinby to the Saccarappa blacksmith shop. And, despite the same lingering myth, it was discovered that Deputy Parker had not entered the blacksmith shop at all, but that Joseph Drew had exited the shop, attacked the law officers, and brutally, viciously, and fatally assaulted Deputy Ebenezer Parker without cause or justification. A dramatic story was uncovered that told of the heroic effort of Richard King, who desperately tried to save his dying friend. And, more truth was revealed as to the vain but thorough effort – despite myth and legend

214.

– to afford Joseph Drew a fair and thorough trial, and the extraordinary and futile appeal to save his life from the gallows. Finally, documents were located which served to narrow down the location of a "long Parker lot" where it is believed that Deputy Parker was laid to rest, in a family plot of graves, in what was then Cape Elizabeth.

The mission of the Historian's Inquiry into locating the final resting place of Cumberland County Sheriff's Deputy Ebenezer Parker had always intended to uncover the truth, dispel the myths, and discover the facts and information that would serve as evidence to assist in the final determination of the location of Ebenezer Parker's grave. As long as there was more information to trace, research, and follow, the Historian's Inquiry continued. As of December 2022, no further documents or information has been located and the likely location of Parker's grave has been determined. All information found during the Historian's Inquiry was then turned over to the current Sheriff of Cumberland County Maine, Sheriff Kevin Joyce. And, as this book goes to press the official results of the ground penetrating radar scan are still anticipated. What further and future action may or may not come as a result, is up to Sheriff Joyce and the Trustees of the Mount Pleasant Cemetery.

Although hard factual evidence may, or may not, be unearthed to prove or disprove the existence of the "long Parker lot" at Mount Pleasant and the inclusion of Deputy Ebenezer Parker in that line of graves, the Historian's Inquiry has been a fruitful one.

For although we may, or may not, ever discover the existence of Deputy Parker's grave the historian's Inquiry was able to unearth the true story – as best as it can be discerned - of the life and death of Ebenezer Parker. Though there may not be a graveside for law enforcement, and Parker descendants, to honor this Fallen Star, there is now a life story that can be known and honored.

The rediscovered life of Ebenezer Parker has revealed a story of a man who was born in Cape Elizabeth and spent some years on a family farm in Gorham. He achieved his coming of age in the time of the American Revolution, and he experienced the excitement and the heartache that came with a local and national struggle for independence from British Tyranny. His story of volunteering to defend his community, his state, and his fledgling nation, at the Seacoast Defenses at Cape Elizabeth on the night of October 18, 1775, tells of his youthful courage. His continued service through the American Revolution proves Parker's patriotism and dedication to democracy. His time on the high seas with his brother John tells of his youthful spirit for adventure. His return home to take the family reins and accept the responsibility of his large family shows him to be a man of responsibility and dedication to his family. His accepting a position as a Cumberland County Deputy Sherriff proves, once again, his courage and commitment to the community. And, his willingness to care for extended family members shows Ebenezer Parker to be a man of honor and responsibility. Though we may, or may not, ever have a grave to honor, we have a story of the man himself that we can now remember and honor. We have a historical truth that has finally been unearthed. A long-enduring myth has finally been corrected, and a true legend of Maine, and American history, has now been correctly delivered to posterity.

Many of the greatest legends in American history are our stories from the pages of Maine's own lore and the true story of the murder of Ebenezer Parker and the trial and execution of Joseph Drew has long been a part of Maine's great legend. Now, a more complete story and corrected record hones that legend to tell a story of one of the most nefarious events in New England history and the current continuation of that story, and the all-out modern-day effort to locate the final resting place of Cumberland County Deputy Sheriff Ebenezer Parker.

***

Acknowledgments

This Historian's Inquiry required an all-out and combined team effort to locate all of the many items of letters, images, documents, maps, articles, deeds, records, and bits of information that were accumulated and reassembled to meet the goals of the inquiry. Many persons or institutions from coast to coast, and from official offices to ordinary individuals, had given time and energy to assist, unearth documents or information, advise, or who assisted in some way or any numerous combination of ways, throughout our nearly five-year search. Sometimes, one of these agencies or individuals simply answered a question via the thousands of telephone or email communications that took place throughout the inquiry. Others may have gone to extraordinary lengths to research or to add to our knowledge or understanding of a person, place, event, or thing. Either way, their assistance to us helped to bring us to where we are today. Below, the author wishes to thank those whose assistance was notable. We hope we did not forget anyone.

Anna Berkes. Collections Development Manager, Jefferson Library. Thomas Jefferson's Monticello, Charlottesville, VA.

Barnstable Historical Society. Massachusetts.

Bob Dodd. President; Cape Elizabeth Historical Preservation Society.

Bowdoin College Library. Brunswick, Maine.

Brian Ackerman, Detective. Cumberland County Sheriff's Office.

Brian Camire, Lt. Colonel. Former Commanding Officer, 133rd Engineer Battalion, Maine Air National Guard, South Portland, ME.

Bridgton Historical Society. Maine.

Cape Elizabeth Historical Preservation Society. Maine.

Clayton Rose, 15th President; Bowdoin College.

Courtney George, Executive Assistant to the Sheriff of Cumberland County Maine.

Cumberland Historical Society. Maine.

Curtis Memorial Library. Brunswick, Maine.

Dr. Richard Kahn. Author & historian.

Durham Historical Society. Maine.
Ellen Planer, Town Clerk. Town of Falmouth, Maine.

Emily Scully, City Clerk. City of South Portland, Maine.

Franklin Delano Roosevelt Presidential Library and Museum. Hyde Park, N.Y.

Fond Du Lac County Historical Society. Wisconsin.

Freeport Historical Society. Maine.

Gorham Historical Society. Maine.

Jay Robbins. Historian.

James Hiltonsmith.

James Rowe. Past President; Cape Elizabeth Historical Preservation Society.

Jamie Rice, Maine Historical Society.

Jane Beckwith. Cape Elizabeth Historical Preservation Society.

Joseph Keefe. National Archives and Records Administration. Waltham, Mass.

Judy Parker Cole. Parker descendant and family historian.

Kelsey Brow. Executive Director. Rufus King Manor Museum. Jamaica, N.Y.

Laurie Chadbourne, Town Clerk. Town of Bridgton, Maine.

Library of Congress. Washington, D.C.

Maine Historical Society. Portland, Maine.

Maine Maritime Museum. Bath, Maine.

Maine State Archives. Augusta, Maine.

Maine State Library. Augusta, Maine.

Mark Swett, Historian. Westbrook Historical Society.

Micheal Comeau. Executive Director, Massachusetts State Archives.

New England Historic Genealogical Society.

New England Historical Society.

National Law Enforcement Officers Memorial and Museum. Washington, D.C.

Nicholas Noyes, Curator/Librarian. Maine Historical Society.

The Officer Down Memorial Page, staff.

Osher Map Library. University of Southern Maine, Portland.

Peter Leech, Application Specialist.

Rebecca Hotaling-Nix. Educator.

Richard D. Brown. Author & Historian.

Ron Romano. Author & Historian.

Ryan F. Waldschmidt. Sheriff. Fond Du Lac County, Wisconsin.

Sally Jordan. Cape Elizabeth Historical Preservation Society.

Scott Leonard. Stroudwater historian.

Standish Historical Society. Maine.

Steve Bromage, Executive Director. Maine Historical Society.

Susan Roberts Norton. Westbrook Historical Society.

Tate Museum. Stroudwater, Maine.

Teri Coviello. Woodfords Congregational Church. Portland, Maine.

The Maine Old Cemetery Association, members.

Tiffany Link, Maine Historical Society.

Truro Historical Society. Massachusetts.

Trustees. Mount Pleasant Cemetery. South Portland, Maine.

Wayne Rivet, Editor. Bridgton News.

Westbrook Historical Society. Maine.

William F. Galvin. Secretary of the Commonwealth of Massachusetts.

William McCarthy, Archivist. Congregational Library & Archive. Boston, Mass.

Yarmouth Historical Society. Maine.

Additional Thanks
From Sheriff Kevin Joyce.

The Cumberland County Sheriff's Office is thankful for the assistance provided by retired history teacher and historian Terence "Terry" Christy of Standish, historian Michael "Mike" Sanphy of Westbrook, and Angela-Berube Gray of Key West FL (formerly of Hiram Maine), for their efforts in researching and uncovering historical information and evidence about the murder of Deputy Ebenezer Parker.

We also would like to recognize Craig Gray, formerly a Hiram Maine stone artist now residing in Key West, Florida, for the acquisition and design of the monument that bears Deputy Ebenezer Parker's name, which is located outside of the Law Enforcement Center on the Cumberland County Sheriff's Office campus.

Lastly, we would be remiss if we didn't thank Lori-Suzanne Dell for her tenacious efforts in working to solve the coldest "cold case" in the history of the Cumberland County Sheriff's Office, the final resting place of our colleague, Deputy Ebenezer Parker.

Bibliography/Sources Used

This is not a full and exact list of all the materials and resources used in the Historian's Inquiry. Many books were borrowed from libraries, read, noted, and returned without a list of their use being made in the early days before the publication of this historian's effort was realized. The following is as best a list as can be reproduced.

An Alphabetical Index of Revolutionary Pensioners Living in Maine. By Charles Alcott Flagg. Sprague's Journal of Maine History. 1920. Dover, Maine.

American Medical Biographies. By H.A. Kelly and W.L. Burrage. Normand, Reddington, Co. Baltimore, MD. 1920.

A History of Cape Elizabeth, Maine. By William B. Jordan. Heritage Books. Bowie, MD. 1987.

A History of Maine: From Wilderness to Statehood. By Marion J. Smith. Bond Wheelwright Co. Freeport, Maine. 1949.

A History of Newspapers in the District of Maine 1785-1820. By Frederick G. Fassett Jr. University Press. Orono, Maine. 1932.

A History of the Congregational Church and Society in Cumberland Maine. By Issac Weston. Brown Thurston Printers. Portland, ME. 1861.

A History of the Town of Gorham Maine. By Josiah Pierce. Foster, Cushing, Bailey, and Noyes Printers. Portland, Maine. 1862.

Babb Families of New England and Beyond. By Jean A. Sargent and Ina Babb Mansur. Limited Copy Manuscript. Laurel, MD. 1987.

Captain Ben's Book. By Captain B.J. Willard. Lakeside Press. Portland, Maine. 1895.

Chapters in the Early History of Cape Elizabeth, Maine. By William B. Jordan. The University of Maine Press. Orono, Maine. 1953.

Copy of the Original Records of the Proprietors of Falmouth, 1718-1826. Edited and Printed by F.A. Gerrish. 1861.

Descendents of Edward Small of New England. Vols I & II. By Laura A.W. Underhill. Riverside Press. Cambridge, Mass. 1910.

Diseases In The District of Maine 1772-1820. By Richard J. Kahn. Oxford University Press. New York, N.Y. 2020.

Early Gravestones in Southern Maine. By Ron Romano. History Press. Charleston, S.C. 2016.

Elijah Kellogg; The Man and his Work. Edited by W.B. Mitchell. Lee and Shepard. Boston. 1903.

For Liberty: The Story of The Boston Massacre. By Timothy Decker. Calkins Creek. Honesdale, PA. 2009.

Genealogical and Family History of the State of Maine. Vol III. George T. Little, Editor. Lewis Historical Publishing company, N.Y. 1909.

Genealogical History of the Quinby Family in England and America. By Henry C. Quinby. The Tuttle Co. Rutland, VT. 1915.

Genealogy of the Early Generations of the Coffin Family in New England. By New England Historical and Genealogical Register. Clapp & Sons. Boston, Mass. 1870.

Genealogy of the Riggs Family, Vol I. By John H. Wallace. John H. Wallace, Printer. New York, N.Y. 1901.

Grandfather Tales of Scarborough. By Augustus F. Moulton. Katahdin Publishing. Augusta, Maine. 1925.

Grandpa's Scrapbook: His Genealogical Columns as Printed in the Deering News from 1894-1904. By Leonard Bond Chapman. Reprint. Heritage Books. Westminster, Maryland. 2012.

Henry Mowatt: Miscreant of the Maine Coast. By Louis Arthur Norton. Maine History Journal. Vol 43, no. 1. January 2007.

History of Colonel Edmund Phinney's Eighteenth Continental Regiment: Twelve Month's Service in 1776 With Complete Muster Rolls of the Companies. By Nathan Goold. The Thurston Print. Portland, Maine. 1898.

History of Durham Maine. By Everett S. Stackpole. Lewiston Journal Company Press. Lewiston, Maine. 1899.

History of Gorham Maine. By Hugh D. McLellan. Smith and Sale Printers. Portland, Maine. 1903.

History of The Westbrook Congregational Church, 1832-1932. By Mrs. Fabius Ray. Printed by H.S. Cobb. Westbrook, Maine. 1932.

Journals of the Rev. Thomas Smith and the Rev. Samuel Deane. By William Willis. Joseph S. Bailey Publishers. Portland, Maine. 1849.

Laws of the Commonwealth of Massachusetts. Printed by Adams and Rhoades. Boston, Mass. January 1808.

Men, Ships, and the Sea. By Captain Alan Villiers. National Geographic Society, Washington, D.C. 1962.

Monograph of the Southgate Family of Scarborough Maine. By Leonard Bond Chapman. Hubbard W. Bryant Publisher. Portland, Maine. 1907.

Old Kittery and Her Families. By Everett S. Stackpole. Lewiston Journal Company Press. Lewiston, Maine. 1903.

Parkers In America, 1630-1910. By Augustus G. Parker. Niagara Frontier Publishing. Buffalo, New York. 1911.

Portland City Guide: 1940. By Works Progress Administration. Forest City Printing. Portland, Maine. 1940.

Portland Directory & Register. By the City of Portland. James Adams Publishers. Portland, Maine. 1827.

Portland Directory & Register. By Nathaniel G. Jewett. Todd & Smith Printers. 1823.

Portland In The Past with Historical Notes of Old Falmouth. By William Goold. B. Thurston and Company Printers. Portland, Maine. 1886.

Portland Neck: The Hanging of Thomas Bird. By Jerry Genesio. Amazon Books. 2010.

Portland's Historic Eastern Cemetery. By Ron Romano. History Press. Charleston, S.C. 2017.

Practical Treatise upon the Authority and Duty of Justices of the Peace, 2nd Ed. By Daniel Davis. Hilliard, Gray, Little & Wilkins Publishers. Boston, Mass. 1828.

Reminiscences of Andrew Hawes of Stroudwater, Maine. By Dr. Allston F. Hunt. Proceedings of the Maine Historical Society: November 16, 1899, to December 19, 1901. Smith and Sale Printers. Portland, Maine. 1902.

Reminiscences of Reverend Edward Payson D.D. By Isaac Weston. Sanborn and Carter Printers. Portland, Maine. 1855.

Reports of Cases Argued and Determined in the Supreme Judicial Court of the Commonwealth of Massachusetts, Vol. IV. By Dudley Atkins Tyng. Little, Brown and Co. Boston, MA. 1865.

Richard Higgins and His Descendants. By Katharine C. Higgins. Published by K.C. Higgins. Worcester, MA. 1918.

Saco Valley Settlements and Families. By G.T. Ridlon Sr. Lakeside Press Printers. Portland, Maine. 1895.

Sketches of the Ecclesiastical History of the State of Maine. By Jonathan Greenleaf. Harrison Gray Publishers. Portsmouth, New Hampshire. 1821.

The Execution of Joseph Drew. By Thomas Shaw. Standish, Maine. 1808.

The Hanging of Ephraim Wheeler. By Irene Q. Brown & Richard D. Brown. Belknap Press. Cambridge, Mass. 2003.

The History of Cape Cod: Annals of the Thirteen Towns of Barnstable County. Vols I & II. By Frederick Freeman. Piper & Co., Publishers. Boston, Mass. 1869.

The History of Portland from 1632 to 1864. By William Willis. Bailey & Noyes Co. Portland, Maine. 1865.

The History of Portland From Its First Settlement. By William Willis. Day, Fraser & Co. Portland, Maine. 1831.

The History of Scarborough from 1633 To 1783. By William S. Southgate. Collections of the Maine Historical Society, Volume III. Brown Thurston Printers. Portland, Maine. 1853.

The Life and Genius of Nathaniel Hawthorne. By Frank P. Stearns. J.B. Lippincott, Co. Philadelphia, Penn. 1906.

The Maine Book. By Henry E. Dunnack. Maine State Library. Augusta, Maine. 1920.

The Maine Register and U.S. Calendar. Edited and Published by F. Douglas and A, Shirley. Portland, Maine. 1821.

This Was Stroudwater, 1727-1860. By Myrtle Kittridge Lovejoy. Anthoenson Press. Portland, Maine. 1985.

Administratrix's Sale. Eastern Argus. Page 4. Vol. ?, No. ? Published by Willis and Douglas Publishers. Portland, Maine. October 27, 1826.

A Son of Bridgton. Bridgton News. Page 2. H.A. Shorey & Sons. Bridgton, Maine. January 5, 1912.

Deaths. Boston Gazette. John Russell Publisher. Boston, Mass. January 28, 1808.

Death Notice. Freeman's Friend. J. Mckown Publisher. Portland, Maine. January 30, 1808.

Death Notice. Gospel Banner and Maine Family Visitant. Augusta, Maine. March 10, 1849.

Death Notice. Portland Advertiser. Portland, Maine. July 9, 1833.

Died. Portland Gazette and Maine Advertiser. Page 3. Published by Isaac Adams. Portland, Maine. January 25, 1808.

Destructive Fire. Eastern Argus. Page 3. Vol. ? No. ? Published by Willis and Douglas Publishers. Portland, Maine. October 7, 1813.

Distressing Fire. Eastern Argus. Vol. 5, No. 229. Page 2. Published by Willis and Douglas. Portland, Maine. January 21, 1808.

Execution. Freeman's Friend. J. Mckown Publisher. Portland, Maine. July 23, 1808.

Governors Proclamation. Eastern Argus, Vol. V, No. 232, page 2. Published by Willis and Douglas. Portland, Maine. February 11, 1808.

Interesting Paper by Hon. William Goold. Portland Daily Press. N.A. Foster & Co. February 3, 1881.

Interesting Trial. Eastern Argus, Vol. V, No. 248, page 3. Published by Willis and Douglas. Portland, Maine. June 2, 1808.

Seventy-Five Dollars Reward. Portland Gazette and Maine Advertiser. Page 4. Published by Isaac Adams. Portland, Maine. May 16, 1803.

Summary of News: Supreme Court. Freeman's Friend. J. Mckown Publisher. Portland, Maine. May 28, 1808.

The Murder of Caleb Parker. Bridgton News. Page 2. H.A. Shorey & Sons. Bridgton, Maine. September 11, 1903.

The History of Westbrook. Numerous articles from the Narragansett Sun. October 3rd, 1895.

The Sea Coast Company. Portland Daily Press. Vol. 32. Portland, Maine. February 23, 1895.

Unfortunate Occurrence. Eastern Argus. Vol. V, No. 228. Page 3. Published by Willis and Douglas. Portland, Maine. January 14, 1808.

Caleb Bradley Diaries, 1799-1861. By Caleb Bradley. In the holdings of the Maine Historical Society. Portland, Maine.

Council Minutes; May 25th, 1808 – May 31st, 1809. Massachusetts Governor's Council of Pardons and Commutations.

History of Portland's India Street Neighborhood. By Julie Larry and Gabrielle Daniello. A report by TTL Architects for the City of Portland's Historic Preservation Office.

Records of the Town of Falmouth, 1728-1773. In the holdings of the Falmouth Town Clerk's Office.

Records of the Cities of South Portland and Cape Elizabeth. In the holdings of the South Portland City Clerk's Office.

Rev. William Gregg Collection, 1850-1913. In the holdings of the Maine Historical Society. Portland, Maine.

Photo/Image Credits

The following is information for the additional photographs, which appear without captions.

Page 41. British Royal Navy Lieutenant Henry Mowatt. Image courtesy digital commons at the University of Maine Library.

Page 44. A lithograph depiction of a Continental Soldier. Image courtesy of the Library of Congress.

Page 51. Marriage record copy card for Ebenezer Parker and Mary Larrabee. Courtesy of Ancestry online.

Page 53. Death record copy card for Esther Parker. Courtesy of Ancestry online.

Page 63. Joseph Drew attacking with a sledgehammer. Original sketch by historian James Rowe.

Page 64. Joseph drew attacking Ebenezer Parker with a club. Original sketch by historian James Rowe.

Page 65. Edited close-up of the front of the blacksmith shop. Image taken in the 1800s. Courtesy of the Westbrook Historical Society.

Page 66. The former home of Dr. Jeremiah Barker at Stroudwater. Date unknown. Courtesy of Old Blue Genes Blogspot.

Page 69. Gilbert Stuart's 1820 Portrait of Dr. Nathaniel Coffin Jr. Image appears courtesy of Danforth Museum, Framingham, MA.

Page 82. Reverend Caleb Bradley. Image appears courtesy of the Maine Historical Society.

Page 83. Edited closeup of Reverend Caleb Bradley's Stroudwater Parish Church on Capisic Street in Portland, Maine. Image appears courtesy of the Congregational Library Archives of Boston.

Page 93. Gilbert Stuart's portrait of Chief Justice Theophilus Parsons. Image courtesy of the Smithsonian American Art Museum.

Page 116. Parker Estate advertisement. November 1808. These advertisements appeared in numerous newspapers in Cumberland County.

Page 125. Digital copy of "The Exemplification of the Case of Joseph Drew with Warrant for Execution." Image appears courtesy of the Massachusetts State Archives.

Page 145. The article of the rabid attack on the Eleazer Parker family at Standish Maine, from the Rutland Weekly Herald, February 1814.

Page 146. Marriage record copy card for the marriage of Mary Larrabee Parker to Joseph Burnell. Image appears courtesy of Ancestry Online.

Page 150. The headstone of Mary Larrabee Parker Burnell at the High Street Cemetery in Bridgton, Maine. Image courtesy of the Bridgton Town Clerk's Office.

Page 166. Headstone of William and Mary "Polly" Parker Riggs in the Saccarappa Cemetery in Westbrook, Maine. Image appears courtesy of the Author.

Page 168. The headstone of Mary Larrabee Parker Burnell at the High Street Cemetery in Bridgton, Maine. Image courtesy of the Bridgton Town Clerk's Office.

Page 173. The preservation work of the Junkin's headstones at Eastern cemetery. Image appears courtesy of Ron Romano.

Page 179. Author and historian Everett Schermerhorn Stackpole as he appears in his book *The History of Durham.*

Page 186. A collection of unsorted documents of the Woodfords Congregational Church or Portland. Image courtesy of the Author.

Page 189. A portion of the article of incorporation of the board of Trustees for Mount Pleasant cemetery in Cape Elizabeth (now South Portland) as it appeared in the Portland Daily Press, August 10th of 1874. Article courtesy of the South Portland Historical Society online.

About The Author

Lori-Suzanne Dell

Lori-Suzanne Dell was educated at La Salle Military Academy in New York, the University of Southern Maine in Portland, and Southern New Hampshire University in Brunswick.

Today, she is a Maine historian who began her career writing feature articles on local Maine histories for various newspapers. She is the administrator of the popular Stories From Maine Facebook page, and she has produced several videos on Maine's illustrious history. *A Fallen Star* is her fifth book.

Lori-Suzanne lectures on many of the remarkable people and events in Maine's history and often teaches courses at Merry Meeting Adult Education in Topsham. Lori-Suzanne makes her home in Brunswick, Maine.

Other Books By Lori-Suzanne Dell

Stories From Maine I & II

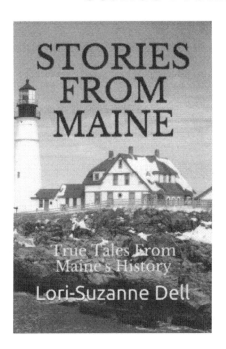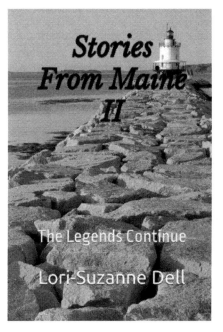

Many of the greatest legends in American history are our Stories From Maine.

These are the incredible true tales from America's 23rd State, which have become forever etched in the monumental granite of our legendary Stories From Maine.

The Quill & The Bayonet

From Uncle Tom's Cabin to Appomattox Courthouse.

Detailing the historic impact of Harriet Beecher Stowe and Joshua Lawrence Chamberlain on the American Civil War.

Texas City.

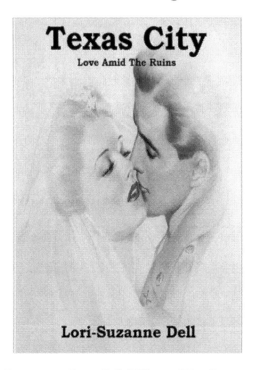

Love Amid The Ruins.

The incredible historic romantic adventure of two young lovers, raised in the cold and withering shadows of the Great Depression, then caught up in the dramatic changes of a world at war, whose relationship survives only to be torn apart by the nefarious designs of another man. John and Katie have one more chance to save their relationship, but first, they have to survive the Texas City Disaster of 1947.

Made in the USA
Columbia, SC
27 April 2023

0a82dd99-6604-4357-92d3-65f75d49d925R01